CRACKING
the PRODUCERS
CODE

CHAD A WADE

ISBN: 0-9740924-7-9

More Heart Than Talent Publishing, Inc.

6507 Pacific Ave #329
Stockton, CA 95207 USA
Toll Free: 800-208-2260
www.MHTPublishing.com

FAX: 209-467-3260

Cover art by FlowMotion Inc.

Acknowledgements

Ever since I hit the pinnacle age of nineteen and read *Think and Grow Rich* by Napoleon Hill, my life has taken a drastic turn of direction. I have always had the mindset of an entrepreneur, even as a young child. I am grateful for that, and would like to give a heartfelt thanks to my parents for teaching me that mindset. They taught me from an early age the importance of entrepreneurship and the rewards that are brought from it. My mother has taught me patience and is a constant source of knowledge and light in my life. My father has taught me a strong work ethic and a persistent drive to succeed. Without the two of them I wouldn't have been able to accomplish what I've done in my life. I want to thank them for believing in me and continuing to offer their unconditional love!

I want to thank my mentor Bob Snyder. He has created and molded me to become the businessman and person that I am today. Bob, I am a carbon copy of you. Everything that I am, everything in this book, all of the information you have collected over the years, you have shared with me, and I am now sharing with everyone in this book. I would have never made it in this industry if not for you. Thank you for your consistent encouragement and belief in me, even when I didn't believe in myself. You are a man of integrity and great value!

My heartfelt thanks to Jim Piccolo, a great mentor who has always believed in me and showed me how to be a good leader! Thank you for creating opportunities. Napoleon Hill says, "The story of practically every great fortune starts with the day when a creator of ideas and a seller of ideas got together and worked in harmony." You are this creator! I will never forget a presentation at the Old Spaghetti Factory when you were speaking in the front of the room and addressed the crowd, saying, "I will bet anyone any amount of money that Chad Wade will be a multimillionaire someday." It is that level of belief in me that has inspired me to work harder.

Jeffrey Combs, a dear friend, mentor and collaborator, I am grateful for your guidance and persistence in helping me to become better in everything that I do! You are a source of wisdom and inspiration.

Erica Combs, your guidance has been invaluable. I am grateful for the spirit you bring to this world and for your counsel through this entire process.

Thank you to Dave Blanchard, a man of great knowledge who has assisted me and guided me through the ups and downs. Thank you for your leadership, friendship, and mentorship!

Thank you to everyone who contributed in the collaboration of this book, from the cover design and artwork to the book layout and editing. Thank you to Jason Secrest for the phenomenal work you did on the flip book and cartoons. Without the assistance of you all I would have never been able to do this!

Lastly, and most importantly I dedicate this book and everything I do to my four children. You are my biggest supporters and have carried me through the most challenging times of my life. I am grateful for your hugs and kisses! You are my WHY!

Foreword

As a twenty-year-plus veteran of direct sales and entrepreneurship, as well as the owner of my seminar company Golden Mastermind Seminars, Inc. and my publishing company More Heart Than Talent Publishing, Inc., I have met hundreds of influential and affluent people. I have been blessed to meet my wife Erica Combs and my best friend Jerry Clark on that journey. However, there is one very unique person I have met who stands out among the many. His name is Chad Wade, and what an example of character and integrity he represents!

I met Chad several years ago when he was just starting his journey. I didn't know what it was then, but I noticed a unique quality about him. I said to him, "It's always the least likely that is the most likely." He looked at me, not sure of what I meant. Well, Chad went on to become a top income earner in his company, a great leader who has developed many six-figure income earners.

What I feel sets Chad apart from many other great leaders is his desire to see others succeed and the courage he possesses to tell it like it is with integrity. I don't just consider Chad a great client, I consider him a great role model and a great friend to my wife Erica and myself. Chad, thank you for enriching our lives!

Jeffery Combs
President and Founder
Golden Mastermind Seminars, Inc.

We live in a time when pervasive purveyors of the new age "Millionaire Magic Doctrine" suggest that a fantasy fairy will somehow grant all of our wishes if we only visualize what we want with enough intention. While others spend valuable time fantasizing about what it will be like when they are rich, Chad became rich.

In a recent survey conducted by the American Psychological Association, we discovered that 75% of this nation is living in stress. Most of this stress is caused by financial challenges which are all too often driven by unmet expectations – the difference between dreams about being rich and financial realities.

In a recent conversation, I asked Chad, "What was the most important lesson you learned while traveling on this journey?" He replied, "Learning to surrender." Chad's answer spoke volumes. Great leaders like Chad live in the NOW. They visualize only to be instructed – to create mentally what needs to be created in reality. They do not go to this "sacred space" to escape and avoid the rigors of life. They do not want to be rich so they can have a life of ease. They want to know how to lift, build, and serve others by contributing value to world – and learn they do!

Once the ideas are created mentally, and an abundant universe willingly participates when one has this intention, they rush back to the NOW and tenaciously execute on the vision – they take action. Chad learned early that vision without action is fantasy and action without vision is just boring, mundane, repetitious work. He knows that if we want to enjoy the blessings that come from the law of abundance, we must be willing to surrender to the principles that govern this law and action is one of the key principles. Chad is definitely a man of action.

Chad's book will provide you with a step-by-step action plan for becoming a producer and creating real wealth. Surrender to the words, take the actions recommended, discover your genius and become rich in reality. This book is not just filled with good ideas it is a tested and proven treasure map and now it is yours!

Dave Blanchard
CEO, The Og Group, Inc.
www.ogmandino.com

CRACKING
the PRODUCERS
CODE

Contents

CRACKING
the PRODUCERS
CODE

Creating Your Journey

Why Network Marketing and Direct Sales?

When I first got started in the network marketing and direct sales industries, I thought success was going to be easy. I found out that it wasn't easy; it was simple. "Easy" is sitting on your butt waiting for success to come to you; "simple" is following the small steps over and over again, which, if followed correctly, will almost guarantee your success. I tried everything under the sun, and nothing ever worked until I discovered the secret code to creating success. Over the years, I worked in six different network marketing, direct sales and multilevel companies before I was able to find true success. Six companies, and I hadn't accomplished any real success in any of them! The sole reason for this book is that I don't want you to have to go down the same long, arduous road and multiple companies before you're able to find true success as well.

When I was nineteen years old, I read a book that absolutely changed my life. It is the holy grail of this entire industry, and it paved the way for how I've created my life and my business. This gold mine is *Think and Grow Rich* by Napoleon Hill. At this point in my life, I had just returned home from donating two years of my life serving local communities in Louisiana and had resumed the same job I'd always had, working in the local dry cleaning business that my family owned. I would spend my days pressing people's shirts and dealing with angry customers, but now I was spending my nights trying to figure out a better way of life for myself. It was at this point that I realized that I deserved more out of life then the traditional J-O-B. It was time for me to take control of my own life and create success.

For more than a decade, I have dedicated my life to pursuing success in the market of free enterprise and cracking the elusive producer's code. Because of my ability to follow the leaders and creators who have paved the path before me,

I've been able to create phenomenal success in this great world of free enterprise. If you follow what I share with you in this book, you will also be able to create that same level of success. It's not a matter of *will* the system work for you, it's will *you* do the work? I subscribe to the philosophy of "Do it wrong enough long enough to get good," but since I continue to carbon copy the people who are getting results, everything I share with you comes from a collaboration of all of my mentors over the years: Napoleon Hill, the author of *Think and Grow Rich*; Anthony Robbins, *Personal Power II;* Bob Snyder, Jim Piccolo, Dave Blanchard, Jeffery Combs, and every other author of any book or audio series I've ever listened to or read… which number in the thousands. Thank you, thank you, thank you! I wouldn't be here or be the person I am without you and your inspiration.

Creating Your WHY

Before I get into the nitty-gritty of how to crack your own production code, let's explore what I truly feel is absolutely, unequivocally the most important proponent of whether or not you will succeed or fail in your business: your WHY.

Why are you here? *Why* did you decide to join your particular company? What are you hoping to get out of the game of free enterprise? You must know and resonate so deeply with your why that failure never even becomes an option. Your why will be 80 percent of your success! If you're not really sure what your why is, then it's time to figure it out. Is it just for the money, or is it what the money will do for you? If that's the case, then you define what the underlying benefit is and define why it's so important for you to realize it.

Let's start out with an exercise. I want you to grab a pen, piece of paper, and a timer. Set that timer for twenty minutes and then write. Write and write and write… don't think about what to write or why you're writing something, or what you're going to do after you finish writing. Just write for twenty solid minutes. Don't lift your pen; don't look at the timer; just write. Let yourself become connected in this particular moment of time. Don't worry about what you're writing or what it means. You might be writing about items as trivial as breakfast cereals; however, as time goes on in this exercise, you'll be surprised at what begins to pour out of your soul onto that piece of paper.

When you're done with the exercise, stop and think about how you feel. What things did you write about? Are you surprised by what you wrote about? Read through what you wrote. Was it difficult for you to write the entire time? Were you able to allow yourself to connect with that moment and allow whatever was inside of you to come out? If so, this is the beginning of your why. Allow yourself to pinpoint what specifically you want and why you want to do it. It could be for your family, your children; you might desire to be a mentor, open a shelter, become a leader... whatever the reason, allow yourself to now connect with it.

Get a 3 x 5 index card and write down your why. Now, put it in your wallet, and every single morning pull out this card and read it. In addition to this, post it everywhere. Allow yourself a few moments to reconnect with your why, and then start your day with the knowledge and foundation of why you're working so hard to create what you're creating.

For example, my why is my four beautiful kids. My why is to make money a nonissue; to never have to say "I can't afford it"; to know that every day that I get up I get to live by the phrase, "I get to, I choose to, I want to"; to prove that my own philosophy can work so that I can share it with others to impact their lives; to impact others on such a level that they thank God they met me.... To have at impacted at least one person to a level that they name their next child after me... just kidding!

Here's another exercise. Tonight, as you fall asleep, I want you to create a feeling from the tip of your nose to the bottom of your toes of what it would feel like to create the success you desire, to win the awards you dream of, to impact others, to drive the car that you want, to own the home of your dreams, to be able to provide for your family in a way that you never thought was possible. I don't want you to just picture the feeling in your *head*, I want you to own what it would *feel* like. Feel what it would be like to capture all of your success, to capture the respect of others, to make as much money as you desire, and to teach others to duplicate this process. Imagine being able to assist others to never have to think about money ever again. Feel this with every fiber of your being, every ounce of your soul! Fall asleep to that feeling; your subconscious mind will work on this the entire time you're asleep, and you'll wake up with the same feeling you fell asleep to. Your subconscious mind doesn't know the difference between a penny and a million dollars, and it doesn't know the difference between a created feeling in your body versus one that is real. You require the assistance of your subconscious mind to go to the next level.

Now that you have connected with your why, I want you to define what you're going to do with it once you've achieved it. If your why is time freedom, what are you going to do with your time after you've earned it? How are you going to give back and invest your time when you have more of it? If your why is more money, how are you going to invest that additional money when you have more of it?

The Importance of Goals

Once you've become extremely familiar with your why, then it's time for you to create specific goals for yourself. Goals are the building blocks to measure and exceed your own personal success. Write down these goals and be very specific with them. An unwritten goal is only a wish. Napoleon Hill said, "Whatever the mind of man can conceive and believe, it can achieve." If you don't write it down, how can you expect to conceive it so that you can believe it, so that you will achieve it? When creating your goals, start with the end in mind. Thinking back to my childhood, I remember looking at the many different cereal boxes and doing the mazes on the back. I discovered that if you start at the beginning, you have a good chance of not making it through the maze, but if you start at the finish and work back to the start, you guarantee success.

I'd like to share a personal example. In December of 2002 I set a goal to make between $20,000 and $25,000 during the month of January. In January I made $22,000 in profit. Unless I'm an idiot, $22,000 is right in the middle of $20,000 and $25,000. Had I known then what I know now, I would have written down a goal for $75,000! Make your plan, see the end, and then work your plan. Create small attainable goals... and then keep moving the bar up. Allow yourself to take those baby steps, and reward yourself for each accomplishment. With that in mind, you should also have a couple of goals that are so out of this world that you would be embarrassed to tell anyone for fear they would laugh at you! (If you can't dream, please don't expect others to!) But at the same time, set smaller goals so that you have a constant emotional high—so that as your accomplish your goals, you create in your body the feeling of success.

The goals you set should include the following to effectively move you to action:

Goals must be big. There is a saying, "If the dream is big enough, the facts don't count." Another says, "If your **why** is big enough, the **how** will take care of itself." You will find the truth of these statements through your own experience.

Goals must be in writing. A goal not written down is only a wish. Multiple times a year I reflect and go over the goals I previously had and set new ones for the upcoming month, quarter, and year. I write down these goals and hang them in a place where I can see them every single day.

Goals must be specific and measurable. This way, you can stay on track, and if you fall behind, you know that some adjustments are in order. Make sure that you hold yourself accountable and follow through with tracking your goals and their progress. This is the only way you'll be able to find areas that require improvement.

Goals must have both a start date and a completion date. This is the best way to create a compelling sense of urgency to drive you to complete the simple daily tasks that, if repeated over time, will lead you to victory.

You must include the action steps necessary to accomplish your goals. Set your plan into action with the knowledge that you may have to make some adjustments along the way. If your required action steps are not keeping you current with the time frame you have established for your goal's completion, then increase your action steps. If this is too overwhelming, then push your completion dates out a bit. This doesn't mean you have failed. The important thing for you to remember is that you will accomplish more, grow more, and become more by setting and working towards your goals than if you don't. Goals provide you with a clear target to shoot for, and with practice you will learn to hit the bull's-eye every time.

If you haven't noticed, cracking the proverbial producer's code isn't simply a numbers game. It encompasses so many other facets in your life that you must find a way to be congruent before you'll be able to crack through your own producer's code. With that in mind, I want to talk about the journey you're now on. A huge portion of it is your own personal development. I believe personal development is why we're here on this planet. I believe that we are here to grow, learn, and progress. I believe that you're going to earn your place in your particular company and in the world as a whole as you perfect this process of becoming. It is critical that you become so familiar with your goals and your why that you will not give up!

Information, Motivation, and Evaluation

You are working on becoming the person of your dreams. It's important to visualize this and visualize a better life for yourself. We are constantly progressing; it is up to each of us whether this is a forward progression or the opposite. To assist you with the path of forward progression, I have found that there are three activities that are vital to integrate into your daily life. Just like food and water, you require a daily dose of :

1) Information
2) Motivation
3) Evaluation

As you strive for constant and never ending improvement, you will begin to develop a love of learning. It can be difficult at first, but create a goal for yourself and make sure that you're learning something new every single day. I've always been told that you've got to learn to love the things you have to do. I have developed a strong love of learning and of reading personal development books — so much so that I feel like my day isn't complete if I haven't dedicated a piece of my day to this action. If learning is going to assist you to become a better you, then you will have to dig in and learn to love learning.

Every day, set aside time for your education. Many times, this can be accomplished while you're doing other things. You can listen to CD programs while getting ready in the morning or before bed at night. Every day when I work out I listen to motivational CDs on my iPod. You can listen to motivational CDs during your morning commute or while you're getting ready in the morning. The only excuse for not turning your automobile into a university on wheels is that you're not disciplined enough to turn off the music or the radio and plug in something that will assist you to become the person of your dreams. I've often said that I've gotten most of my business education and personal development while sitting in traffic. (Mix it up with some good rock n' roll, though; otherwise you'll go crazy!)

When you're listening to these CDs, try to pay attention to what the author is trying to tell you. If something really grabs you, hit pause, rewind it, and listen to it again. Allow yourself to have moments every day when something jumps out at you and you're able to really connect to what you just heard.

In addition to the CDs you listen to, how about the books you read? My bedroom and office are filled with books to assist me with my business, my personal development, and my mindset. I've got a membership card to everyone of my local bookstores. What about the events that you attend and the people you hang around with? I've become very selective with my time and with whom I spend my time. The books, the audio programs, the seminars, and the people you associate with are all primary influences that can shape and mold you into your very best person. Remember this very valuable formula: information, motivation, and evaluation.

Let's move on to *motivation*. Motivation is extremely important. We all require a daily dose of motivation. Motivated people get things done. There are definitely things you can do to improve how motivated you are. It's just like working out. I can tell you from experience that, regardless of how much I want to get into shape, I have limits on how fast I can run or how many reps I can do without some really pumping, motivating music to fire me up. The right music brings the right energy, which motivates me to work out harder. The same is true of the right motivational topics, the right motivational books, and the right motivational seminars. They'll fire you up so that you have the added oxygen necessary to build your business in the face of adversity. Without that added oxygen called motivation, you could very easily come up short and quit the path that you're on when it gets a little bit rocky. So make the effort to consume the audios, the books, and the events that will assist you to succeed and enable you to have the staying power required to sustain you on the road to riches.

There will be days when you feel down or disappointed. Some days, instead of progressing forward, you'll actually digress a little. This is why it is so important to integrate a piece of motivation into your life every single day. If I had paid attention to those negative days and not allowed myself to grow and move on from them, I would have never been able to create the level of success I have experienced in my business.

The last part of this formula is *evaluation*. Never overlook evaluation. Every morning, you've got to set time aside to evaluate and plan your day so that you use your time most effectively. Next, you should set time aside every night to evaluate your performance and take inventory of what you've done that day. There are too many people that get involved in direct sales or network marketing and never do anything of consequence. The reason is pretty simple: in their own mind they are working their business to death, but unfortunately, in reality they aren't working at all. They're spending all of their time getting ready to get ready instead of DOING! This is why it is so critical to measure your daily activities.

I am consistently evaluating my life, my daily schedule, my activities, and my production so that I can track the progression I'm experiencing. Don't get me wrong—some days are much harder than others, and it's not always an easy task, but it is extremely vital to evaluate your own performance. *When performance is measured, performance improves.* Evaluation has allowed me to see the areas that require improvement as well as motivates me because I'm able to recognize the areas I'm strong in.

You'll find that there are four main activities in a direct sales/network marketing business: connect with people, tell the story, build for events, and follow-up. It's really that simple. We'll cover each of these activities in great detail later in the book, but for now, be forewarned, if your marketing activities aren't focused on these four ideas, you will not make any money.

If you're looking for a hobby, not a cash-flowing business, then go get a kitty cat or a kite. That's why daily evaluation is so important. When you take personal inventory each night of what you did that day, you won't be fooled or tricked into thinking you're working when really you're not. Always remember: *When performance is measured, performance improves.* It's a simple formula.

Information, motivation, and evaluation... these are the three daily critical components required for you to realize your dreams.

Developing a Winner's Mindset

Next, we'll cover developing a winner's mindset. It's been said that winners never quit, and quitters never win. I want you to predetermine each morning that you're going to have an amazing day. Predetermine that quitting is not an option and that you're going to build your business until you're done. Build it until, and predetermine to succeed.

Failing is not an option—this requires you to focus on positive things. When you focus on the positive, you'll attract positive things to you because you have invited them into your life. Over time, your subconscious will find a way to manifest your dreams, and the money and success will come. Too many people have the "have, do, be" mentality. They think that if they *had* a million dollars, they would *do* those things that millionaires do, and then they would truly *be* happy. I suggest you turn this around and develop a "be, do, have" mentality. If you'll *be* the person you want to become, then you'll *do* what that person would do, and you'll *have* everything in life that you could possibly want.

This requires you to take personal responsibility for your business and the decisions you make. This means that you take ownership of your business. If your business is thriving, take credit; if your business is failing, take responsibility. Remember that every experience brings with it opportunities for personal growth and development.

These are just a few ideas to keep you on track and progressing towards the realization of your dreams. Commit yourself to the process, and don't get discouraged if you have a character building day once in awhile. Every person in network marketing started at the same place. We all had our first day, we all had our first month, and we all had our first year. Fortunately, you have this book and many other tools to set you on the proper course. So, pay attention and take seriously the information you receive in this book, and then apply what you learn by taking extreme, full-force action. Daily participation in positive actions will enable you to implement these strategies for greater success. Results follow activity. If

you don't act, you're never going to achieve.

Napoleon Hill acquired an amazing opportunity over the course of about twenty years or so. He personally interviewed and studied the success habits of over 500 of the wealthiest people in the world, and he documented his findings and created a road map for success that is available today. It's all there in his book *Think and Grow Rich*. I suggest that you read it, reread it, and do so every year. I've personally read it over 300 times and will continue to do so every year for the rest of my life.

If you get nothing else out of my book, at the very least take this one bit of advice. Buy, *Think and Grow Rich* by Napoleon Hill read it, and apply his information. Then I want you to read it again and again and again. You get the point! When I die, I'm first going to find my grandfather, and next I'm going to find Napoleon Hill and thank him for changing my life.

One of the little gems I've pulled out of his observations is this: the story of practically every great fortune starts the day when a creator of ideas and a seller of ideas get together and work in harmony. That's what happens in free enterprise. Your company creates the ideas. You are contracted as the seller of those ideas, and when you work together, great, astronomical success can be created. So start by dreaming big, and then work a plan towards the realization of those dreams.

At this point, you've allowed yourself to connect with your why, and you've set some goals for yourself. We've discussed the importance of daily information, motivation, and evaluation. It's now time for you to begin to create financial success in your business enterprise.

NOTES

A Proven Plan of Action

Starting Your Business

This next part of the book outlines steps for getting your business started. One of the most basic principles in network marketing and direct sales is expanding your network of friends and acquaintances. Many small businesses, in particular Web-based businesses, model their business plan after this idea. What is the fastest way to circulate information? Word of mouth! Word of mouth is, in its simplest form, the most powerful mode of advertising and getting exposure to your enterprise. You'll find as you get started in your business that word of mouth will become one of your best friends!

From the starting gate, you have to act as your own instructor and facilitator. Always remember that *you* will be your greatest cheerleader. One big mistake I commonly see people make is comparing their results with other people in their enterprise. You can't expect the same results as the top income earner in your company, nor should you expect the same results as the person who isn't doing anything with their business.

Be realistic about your own expectations. When you've been working towards your goals, if results aren't happening as quickly as you had hoped, that's okay. Maybe what's required is that you reevaluate the time and resources you currently have available to dedicate to your business. For example, if you work full time, you can't expect yourself to have the same results as someone who isn't working at all. You don't have to ignore your current responsibilities in order to succeed. Like everything else in life, this is a game of balance. This is why it is important to take your business extremely seriously and not treat it like a hobby. If you take the little amount of time to organize your weekly and daily schedule, and then if you follow through and hold yourself accountable to that schedule, you'll find that your production level will increase. This is a great starting point for measuring your own personal success.

Getting to Know and Quickly Becoming Independent from Your Mentor

The majority of companies will assign you to a mentor, or a coach. This might be the person who introduced you to the business or a senior advisor in the company. However, almost every company also has systems already in place. Systems allow you to free up time, ensuring that the people who sign up under you gets proper training while you remain focused on personal sales.

With this in mind, in the beginning you'll need to meet with your mentors. When you start your business, make sure you secure the names and phone numbers of those individuals who will receive income from the sales training required for your certification or who will be receiving income through residual sales from the teams you are building. Get to know them as quickly as possible. They have a financial interest in your success and will act as guides to walk you through the rest of the training process.

Having a mentor can shorten your learning curve and drive you to create greater profitability in your business. Think about it: can you name one successful individual out there who doesn't have a mentor? *Always* find a mentor. Find someone who inspires you, someone who can counsel you to become more than you thought you could be.

Your "network" will determine your "net worth." We should all strive to surround ourselves with the very best of the best so they can call us forward. Take a look at the top five people that you surround yourself with. Now, take a look at their income; I can almost guarantee that your incomes are in similar brackets.

The person who enrolled me in my last venture was not the mentor I was looking for, so I looked around and found the top income earner, and I found ways to assist that person until they listened to me and took me under their wing. I assisted that person until they had a reason to reciprocate and assist me. Because

of the law or reciprocity, I knew that by finding ways to serve this leader, ultimately there would be opportunities for this person to serve me.

An assignment: Go through all of the potential trainings you can and then go back to your mentor, show them your plan of action, and ask them for some guidance. If you approach your mentor with that type of attitude, they will give you all the time that you require. If, on the other hand, all you have is a weak list of questions, your mentor will know that you have not done your due diligence or taken your training seriously.

The second reason for making a quick introduction to your mentor is additional support. Many times all you'll require in this business is a workout buddy. It's nice to have someone to bounce ideas off of or pick you up when you haven't had a great day. In other words, you'll create a "mastermind alliance." This is another concept from *Think and Grow Rich*. (Have you gotten the hint that this is a book you really want to pick up?)

It may be that you just require some third party credibility when a potential marketer or customer requires a gentle nudge in their business. Regardless of the support you seek, these individuals have the responsibility to assist you.

The last reason to get to know your mentor is that often certification in your company must happen through them. Your mentor has a vested interest in assisting you to succeed. Each time you advance in the program, you'll be doing so with your next-in-line mentor. So, get on the phone, introduce yourself, and get to work building your empire.

After you've established relationships with your mentors, you'll want to quickly become system-dependent, not mentor-dependent. Be sure to go through your company's training program. Once you've completed this training, you'll have earned the right to schedule time with your mentor and get all your questions answered.

Until you've completed your company's training program, any time you demand of your mentor will cost you both time and money. You will have violated the first lesson in this book: becoming system-dependent instead of mentor-dependent.

The person who enrolled me in my last enterprise told me that they didn't have time when I called them to ask for assistance. This was the best thing that could have happened to me. It required me to get out there and just do it myself!

If you don't learn to follow the system early on, then there is a pretty good chance that you won't require others to follow it, and this will cost you time and money. Your downline will become dependent on you, and you won't have time to increase your personal business, which of course is the lifeblood of every successful marketer.

Independence is crucial. The last thing you want to do is create this business on someone else's timeline. Wait for no one! Ingrain this affirmation in your daily thoughts: "If it is to be, it's up to me." Up to *who?* Up to *you.* You're the one who is responsible for your success—not your mentor, not the company, not the government, not alien beings from another world! If it is to be, it's up to YOU. But here is the blessing of being involved with network marketing or direct sales. You may be in business for yourself, but you're not in business by yourself.

Be a Product of the Product

When individuals ask the question, "Do I have to purchase the product to get started?" The answer will always be, "No." To operate in compliance with state and federal authorities, there is no product requirement at any level of most programs. I make this clear. However, if you met someone marketing a product that sounded really great, would you want to purchase it if you knew that salesperson didn't even use it themselves? Absolutely not! Why would you be willing to invest your own money in a product the salesperson doesn't even have enough confidence in to purchase it?

I'll give you a real life example. When I purchased my four-door GMC truck, I purchased it from the fourth salesman I talked to. Why couldn't the previous three salesmen sell me the truck? Because they were selling me on the features not the benefits. They were trying to sell me on the number of cup holders the truck had and the extended warranty plan that I could also purchase. The fourth salesman, who was successful at selling me the truck, owned the exact same truck I purchased. He sold me on the benefits. He sold me on the fact that if I got stuck in some mud in the middle of nowhere I'd be able to get out using the powerful engine and four-wheel drive the truck had to offer because he had been in similar situations. He could speak to me with passion and integrity. The same thing applies to anything you do in life.

I have spent years in the direct sales and multilevel marketing industries, and I want the people I work with to have the best possible chance for success. I always ask them, "Do you want to start fast or slow?" How would you respond if asked that question? I have always wanted to achieve success in the shortest time possible, and I believe that is true for most individuals. So I have chosen to do what successful mentors have done before me. I purchased the product. The reason is simple: As a marketer, I could not in a good conscience attempt to sell a product that I did not own myself.

I also realized the credibility I would gain with my potential customers or recruits by developing my own merchandise savings testimonials. Your products are incredible and the fact that you own them and use them and have personal experience with their benefits will enable you to make more sales! After all, you cannot sell from an empty wagon unless you are selling the wagons. Build your own testimony with the products your company produces.

You have to lead by example. It's all part of becoming a product of the product. I don't know of any good marketer that in good conscience has sold a product they didn't purchase and use on a regular basis. Doesn't it sound a little hypocritical to sell something you don't even own?

If you're going to succeed financially in this industry, you've got to be committed to the wealth cycle that you'll learn about in this book. The wealth cycle starts with simply selling your product and then taking a portion of your proceeds to build your business even more.

Creating Your Business Plan

The next step in getting started is to create a business plan and set goals. Just like a goal to exercise each day a little earlier, start with the end in mind. Get a clear vision of what you want in your business, and then create a plan to realize it. As a part of your business plan, create a mission statement that you can read daily. This will remind you of your purpose.

Include in your business plan what you desire to accomplish, your objectives, your dreams, as well as a specific plan of action to achieve them. Determine how many hours a week you'll put into your business, what lead sources you will use, and what method of recruiting you'll employ. Set goals for how many guests you're going to have at your presentations, how many presentations you'll have each week, and how many sales you're going to generate through these actions. You'll also want to set specific goals for advancement in your company's certification. Through the process of setting and meeting these goals, you will get a very good feel as to where you're going to be financially in one month, three months, and a year from now.

Simple daily tasks repeated over time will lead you to victory. Always include the action steps necessary to accomplish your goals. List the obstacles you're going to have to overcome. List the skills and specialized knowledge that you may require in order to reach your goals. Also, make sure you list the benefits of attaining your goal, and keep the dream your center of focus. That way you won't waste time thinking about all the obstacles in your way.

Visualize yourself succeeding. Put your plan into action with the knowledge that you may have to make a few adjustments along the way. If your required action steps aren't keeping up with the time frame you've established for the completion of your goal, then you increase your action steps. Hold yourself accountable at a higher level to get the results you're searching for.

If this seems too overwhelming, you can push your completion dates out a bit. This doesn't mean that you've failed. The important thing to remember is that you will grow more, you will accomplish more, and you will become more by setting and

working towards goals than if you don't set any goals. Goals give you a very clear target to shoot for. With practice, you're going to learn to hit the bull's-eye every time. Remember the success formula: information, motivation, and evaluation. Each of these three steps works beautifully with goal setting and completion.

Having a sound business plan is integral to keeping you on task. It is important to realize that it will also change as you continue to grow and build your business. I also recommend setting aside specific time at least once a quarter to analyze your current business plan and make adjustments and new goals for the next quarter. Again, make sure that this plan is written down and that you hang it in a location where you will see it and read it on a consistent basis.

Managing Your Business Time

The next step is learning how to manage your nonnegotiable business time. Purchase an appointment book, and then, based on your business plans, schedule yourself to work your business. If you've committed to work ten hours a week, then work ten hours each and every week. Consistency is the key. Ten hours a week might be broken down as follows: two hours on Tuesday, three hours on Thursday, and five hours on Saturday. If this is your plan, stick to it.

Don't let anything or anyone interfere with your plan. Don't kid yourself into thinking that you can work extra hard one week and then take the following week off. Any momentum your business has gained will be lost, and you'll have to start all over. That's not only going to frustrate you, but it's also going to frustrate your mentor.

To maintain balance in your life, schedule nonnegotiable family time, time for employment, time for self-improvement, time for exercise, time for church responsibilities, and so on. However, schedule it as *nonnegotiable* time. It's the only way to maintain balance and be committed to the process of getting things done.

Distractions *are* going to come along. Friends will drop by; they'll call and invite you to go to the ballgame or suggest that you get together on Wednesday night.

Whatever they're suggesting, don't think of it as an offer; consider it a distraction. If your schedule is booked with your business activities, well, then you're going to have to take a pass. My dad always told me, "You can pay now and play later, or you can play now and pay later." I'd rather pay now and play later... because I'll be able to play at one heck of a higher level than I would have if I'd played first instead of working.

NOTES

The Basics

Creating Your Work Space

Set aside a specific place for your office. Find a place in your home that is as free from distractions as possible. This might be a bedroom, the dining room, or a home office. It's important to have a place you can call your own. This way, your mindset will change when you enter that area, and you'll be able to adjust between home and business with greater speed and efficiency.

Organize that area to meet your requirements and those of your business. Purchase a phone with a mute button, a speaker, and a flash button. A headset will definitely make your life easier. Your phone is one of your most important tools; don't be afraid to spend a little bit of money to get a good one. A good phone will increase productivity and sales.

Call your phone carrier and request three-way calling. This is a must! This enables you to talk to two separate individuals at separate locations at the same time. For example, while your guest is on the phone, you'll be able to conference in your mentor or business buddy to assist you with questions and credibility, or you can conference your guest into a live presentation call. The cost of this service is minimal, but it's very important to your success.

Make sure you have an answering machine, or better yet, voicemail added by your local telephone carrier. You want people to be able to reach you or leave you a message.

Call waiting is another valuable tool. It's a bit of an irritant at times, but it can make you a fortune. Call waiting allows you to respond to incoming calls while you're already on the phone with somebody else. Fewer missed calls equal more money.

Purchase a good quality tape recorder with jacks for mike and playback, automatic recording level control, counter, and pause. This will allow you to record recruiting calls and then play them back on a tape recorder through your phone for your guests, rather than three-way calling into the line and incurring additional expense.

These little tools will assist you to record training or conference calls with your mentor and play them back for your guests. You can also record yourself making prospecting and follow-up calls so that you can listen to them later. You can use this as a gauge for self-improvement. Your mentor can also listen to your calls and give you feedback.

Always look for ways to improve. As you gain more skill, suddenly you'll discover that your leads have gotten better. So, if a little recording device can assist you to critique yourself or enable your mentor to give you some counseling, this is going to make you more money.

Sometimes you may be required to fax documents or receive them. When doing transactions, a fax machine becomes mandatory. A fax machine will enable you to provide your prospects with information more quickly. Your mentor will be able to fax you updates when necessary. You don't have to spend a lot of money; I recommend purchasing a plain paper fax with a handset that can send and receive legal size paper. If you can't afford your own fax machine initially, you can always use the fax machine at Kinko's.

Marketing Materials

Think about how you're going to market your business. What kind of marketing materials will you have in your home office? Consider marketing materials like audio CDs and DVDs from your company or product brochures you can leave with your guests after their initial exposure to your business. Some marketing materials assist you to create leads; some marketing materials communicate your message in a follow-up situation. Just make sure you are familiar with the marketing materials that are available from your company.

I'm always prepared with marketing materials from my company. I never know when I'm going to meet someone who is interested in my opportunity and I want to be as prepared as possible to share information effectively. I keep folders in the trunk of my car with brochures and CDs ready to go in case I need them. I also always make sure that I have my company's marketing information with me whenever I meet with a potential prospect. Having information handy shows a level of professionalism and preparedness. One piece of advice, though: I don't ever give out a piece a marketing material to someone without getting their name, email address, and telephone number first.

Computers

Having a computer with an email account is no longer optional. It's an absolute must—you'll find that the majority of your communication takes place via email.

With a computer, you'll also be able to send valuable marketing information to your guests and customers. This is one tool that's going to make a big difference in your productivity. You don't have to go overboard; protect your financial resources at all costs so that you have the financial oxygen to build your business profitably. If you have to wait awhile to acquire a computer, then find other ways to build your business in the meantime. Use the computer at your local library.

When I first started in this industry, I had the most basic computer, and sometimes it worked and sometimes it didn't. I used what I could and built my business with what I had until I was able to upgrade to something more efficient. I now keep a tablet PC with me so that I'm able to host online conferencing sessions with potential prospects and walk through different scenarios with them at anytime. This is extremely effective because I'm able to share the same information with someone irregardless of where they're located.

Don't let *any* obstacle stand in the way of your success. Look for the work-around, figure out what it's going to take, then engage and build your business. For instance, even though I've become pretty familiar with using a computer, there are some things that I just do better with a pen and paper. When it comes to keeping track of my prospects and appointments, I do a whole lot better with 3 x 5 cards. They're cheap and effective. Every time I go through my answering machine I

jot down the information for each person on a different 3 x 5 card. I then use little Post-it® notes to keep track of specific information regarding phone calls and messages I've left for that person.

I also keep a business journal. I do this so that I'm able to keep notes about the business meetings I've been involved in as well as write down any great ideas that might pop into my mind. I typically handle many situations at one time, and by keeping a journal and documenting things I'm able to refer back to it to keep me on track and productive. All too often, I have some fantastic, life-altering idea that I forget before I have the chance to do something about it. Keeping a journal assists me to overcome the problem of selective memory. Reviewing my notebook on a regular basis keeps me on track with my business goals and my business plan.

1-800 Number

Another great resource is setting up your own toll-free number. There are a number of companies out there that you can use to easily and inexpensively set up a toll-free number.

You can prescreen prospects and collect messages using your toll-free number's voicemail. This voicemail box allows opportunity seekers listen to your personal message. When they call in from your ads and listen to your message, if they like what they hear, they'll leave their name and number and request more information. This voicemail service allows you to set up a marketing service where you can prescreen and prequalify prospects 24/7 without having to pick up every live call. Everything goes into voicemail, and you're able to return calls when it's convenient for you.

Here's an example of a voicemail script I have used in the past:

"Hello and thanks for calling. My name is Chad. You're obviously looking for a better way of making money or else you wouldn't have called this number. I know there are a lot of things out there that look good, smell good, but end up being no good. This is not that deal. All I need from you is your name, your phone number, your email address, and the best time to get a hold of you. Either one of my associates or I will get back to you as soon as possible.

Right now, you have no idea what you're saying yes or no to, and I can't assist you unless I have your name, phone number, and email address so I can give you all the business information for you to make a logical business decision. So once again, please leave your information, and we'll get back to you as soon as possible."

At this point in the voicemail, I usually tell a couple of quick success stories about individuals in my enterprise. I don't spend more than two minutes for the entire message.

Scripts

If you're brand-new to this industry and you're not familiar or comfortable with the phone, then some of your best tools are going to be scripts. Check with your company to see if they have some specific scripts regarding your product. I've also included some of the scripts I initially used when I started in this industry, you can find them later on in the book.

Scripts are extremely important because they allow you to prescreen potential customers. You'll want to rehearse these scripts. Read them out loud at least twenty times before getting on the phone with someone. Rehearse them until you are so comfortable with the message that it just flows as naturally as any conversation would. Keep in mind that many of the highest paid individuals in the world are nothing more than professional script readers. (We call them movie stars.) They memorize their lines and then deliver them in a way that is natural, comfortable and believable.

When you print out your script, I suggest that you memorize it word for word so that it flows naturally. Once you've done this, take that script, crumple it up, and throw it away. You don't have to look at it anymore. Once you've mastered it, you will never have to look at it again. From this point forward, you will own the dialogue. It will become yours, and every call will become conversational.

NOTES

_____

_____

_____

_____

_____

_____

_____

_____

_____

_____

_____

_____

_____

_____

_____

_____

NOTES

_____

_____

_____

_____

_____

_____

_____

_____

_____

_____

_____

_____

_____

_____

_____

_____

_____

_____

Become a Leader

Build for and Attend All Company Events

Make sure you build for and attend all local and national events. If you have local training and weekly opportunity meetings in your area, use them. You have a tremendous resource for closing business and training associates. When I first got started in my business, one of the most important pieces of advice I received was to never miss an event.

My mentor used to say that not everyone who attends weekly meetings makes ten thousand a month, but everyone who makes ten thousand a month attends weekly meetings. That's a huge indication of just how important it is to be a participant at these events. I've achieved amazing success over the past years because I have always been willing to show up early and stay late for the weekly meetings.

I can count on one hand how many trainings and meetings I have missed. Become familiar with what is up and coming. Keep a list, and support your local leaders as they host these events. Also, if at all possible, don't go alone. Many of the meetings are held for the sole purpose of exposing guests to your opportunity. You want to pack these meetings with prospects who are hungry for your enterprise's opportunity. The more you pack them in, the more money you're going to make.

When you attend company training calls and meetings, be a participant, not a spectator. If you've had a good week, then the meeting needs you. On the other hand, if you've had a bad week, then you need the meeting. Regardless of the situation, conference calls and meetings are crucial to your business. This is how you'll stay plugged into your support team, and it's also how you develop the skills to present your enterprise's opportunity.

If you don't have local meetings, take the lead and start one. Become a presenter. It will give you and your team members an event to build towards every week. Every guest that you have in the process should be invited to this meeting. This will greatly improve your closing ratios and give you an opportunity to build trust and rapport much more quickly than if you recruit only over the telephone. Seventy-nine percent of all successful sales are made face-to-face! Think about it. People want to feel connected to something bigger than themselves. People want to feel that connection; they want to have a purpose! Being around other people that believe in you and support your goals and aspirations is a must if you are ever to create that reality.

Once a week you can associate personally with those who support your dreams. You can spend time with your leaders and get recharged for the upcoming week. Stay plugged into this plan of action, teach your people to do the same, and your business will grow. If you try to build a business without this, you're in for an uphill climb.

Become a Presenter

Study your company's presenter information and compliance guide. Many companies require you to be a qualified or certified presenter before you'll be allowed to present the business opportunity at a meeting. Remember, facts tell and stories sell! If you don't have your own story, then tell the story of a successful person in your group…and get to work on a story of your own! Apply what you have learned so that you can show the plan without assistance. Practice, practice, practice!

Part of being a great presenter is your professional appearance. It is imperative that your professionalism and desire to succeed in your business is reflected in your appearance. I'm not saying you have to go out and purchase designer suits. However, it is vital to pay attention to your appearance. Make sure that your clothing is clean and pressed. Make sure that it is professional and appropriate. First impressions are important, and your appearance will be crucial in helping a person determine whether or not you're the leader they are looking for. When you present to an audience, everyone out there will be judging your organization and opportunity by your presentation and the manner in which you deliver it. A part of that is your appearance.

Repetition brings definition and confidence. Repetition is the mother of skill! Become confident. Remember this: he or she who holds the marker makes the money. He or she who holds the audience makes a fortune. It's funny to think of my first presentation.... My mentor had been pushing me for weeks to get up in front of the room. I put it off and put it off and would intentionally come to the meetings in jeans to try and get out of it. Fortunately, I have a mentor who doesn't give up that easily and this mentor eventually made me get up, even though I had intentionally attended the meeting in jeans. I will be forever grateful to Bob Snyder for pushing me *way* beyond my comfort zone!

You see, you have super heroes and their sidekicks. For example, let's take Batman and Robin. As long as Batman and Robin are together, they are a kick-butt team. You might even think of Robin as a superhero. I can think of many times that Robin saved the day, but Robin's strength came from his mentor's belief in him. Let's face it, Robin without Batman is just a "wanna be" in tights. Without Batman, Robin and all of Gotham are screwed.

It's okay to be Robin in the beginning, but you want to become Batman as soon as possible. Remember, he or she who holds the marker makes the money, and he or she who holds the audience makes a fortune.

Attend All Major Functions

If you attend all of your company's events, your people will follow your lead. If they attend, their belief level will rise, they will develop a stronger commitment to succeed. When they succeed, you will benefit and your business will prosper, so don't stay home and don't accept excuses for absentees.

If you don't attend events, you might as well pull out a knife and slit your financial throat. First, you never know which event is going to be *your* event. I'll never forget being at one of my company's events. I really couldn't financially afford to be there, and a lot of people in my life were giving me a hard time about joining network marketing and direct sales, but had I not attended that event I would not have created the success I have in the last six years. That event switched something off on the left side of my brain and turned something on on the right side. It's hard for me to explain adequately what I'm trying to get across to you. It's a little like trying to explain what salt tastes like—you have to experience it to understand. Just trust me, be at every event your company sponsors and make sure that everyone who is a part of your team also attends each and every one of those events.

Leaders are expected, not requested, to attend all events. There are only three legitimate reasons for missing an event: 1) you're dead; 2) you're getting married; or 3) you're about to deliver a baby!

Negatives Go Upline; Positives Go Downline

Your business will not be without its challenges or disappointments. This is to be expected. There isn't anything in life really worth working for and achieving if it comes to easily. You will have to pay a price, so anticipate that you will have to go through growing stages along the way. If you feel the urge to negatively vent, take it to your mentor and ask them for assistance in overcoming your particular obstacles. Never spew negatives to your associates. A good leader never does this. Your associates and team members look up to you and expect you to be positive. Negatives from your lips could crush them or create confusion, and we all know that a confused mind quits. Assist them to develop belief in themselves and their opportunity so they can move forward with a clear head. A word to the wise: If you are encountering challenging times, work harder.

I once had one of my upline leaders say, "If this doesn't work out, I'll find another opportunity that will." Up until this point I thought everything in the business was going fine. I ultimately quit this business because my faith had been shaken. My mentor and one of the top leaders questioned the company that I was a part of, and I lost something from that day forward. Once that faith is gone, it can be extremely difficult, if not impossible, to get it back.

I have found that the only way to reverse a negative downward spiral is to double and triple my efforts. Most emotional and financial problems could be solved if we would just put another fifty people into the recruiting process. One surefire way to eliminate all the negatives in your business is to refer back to your why. My why has always kept me grounded, working hard, and out of drama, because I discovered that if your why is big enough, negativity is minimized. Just remember, 80 percent of your success is *why*, and only 20 percent is *how*. If your why is big enough, none of the rest of it matters.

Here is a suggestion. If you have something negative to bring to your mentor, please pull out a piece of your most beautiful stationery and then write an eloquent letter, explaining exactly what you're feeling angry about. Check it for grammatical and spelling errors, seal it in an envelope, and then mail it to yourself. You'll then want to immediately begin working on a solution for that very problem. If done correctly, you'll have a solution before the letter hits your mailbox. This way, you'll become an asset to your organization and not one of those people that sucks the marrow out of your mentor's soul.

One of the most important pieces of advice I have learned from successful businessmen and businesswomen over the years is that whenever you think you have a problem, don't go to your associates and mentors and complain about it. Take the time to investigate why you think it's a problem and then come up with a feasible solution. At this point, if you're not able to take care of it yourself, *then* contact your immediate mentor and bring it to their attention. You will not be wasting their time at this point with needless gossip if you've invested the time to investigate a legitimate problem and come up with a solution.

Conduct Your Own Leadership Calls

By now, you have established yourself as a leader and your team is looking to you for direction. Hosting your own team calls will allow you to be the head of your team. You can more easily identify the up-and-coming leaders in your business, and you can develop an open forum for positive suggestions. Your call should include business-building tips, announcements, recognition, guest speakers, evaluation, and strategy.

As your business continues to grow and get larger everyone will want a piece of your time, and it can be difficult to do that on a one-on-one basis. That is why team calls will become an integral part of your business. This is a great way to keep everyone informed; your team members are able to prepare and come to you with specific questions on these calls, and you're able to work with individuals regarding their specific business with other participants at the same time. You'll come to find that the same questions and needs will come up time and time again, so having a team call allows you to assist many people at the same time.

Every day I have scheduled calls that my team members can log onto and listen to me prospect, and then they're able to ask me specific questions after the calls. I host two calls, one for anyone in my organization, and one specifically for those who are working directly with me. This way, they're system-dependent, not mentor-dependent. It is their responsibility to get on the call, connect with me, ask their questions, and get their answers. If they don't get on the calls, then they lose that opportunity. As your business continues to grow, you'll find it imperative to do this in order to effectively manage your time.

Make it a call that everyone will want to attend, one they can feel a part of. If you don't feel that your team is big enough to have your own call, then plug into your mentor's team call until you have a large enough following, or unite with your mentor to bring your knowledge and training to his or her team call, because Together Everyone Achieves More—TEAM!

NOTES

NOTES

The Recruiting Process -
Become an Expert in Four Things

Learn and Practice the Recruiting Process

You will want to become a master at four simple steps—these basic steps will be repeated over and over to you throughout this book. However, they absolutely cannot be overlooked; they are the foundation of your business. You must become a MASTER at these four steps in order for you to achieve success.

This section is by far the most important part of this entire book. If you're not consistently recruiting new prospects, then your business is moving backwards, your pipeline is going to dry up, and you're going to quit making the big bucks.

Recruiting in its simplest form consists of four actions:

1. Connect with people
2. Tell the story
3. Build for events
4. Follow up

Recruiting is a process; it's not a one-time event. It is a very simple process though, most people overcomplicate it and make it much more difficult than it needs to be. Most people have to see information three to seven times before making any kind of decision. Your job is to educate potential recruits, enabling them to make an intelligent and informed decision about your opportunity. Remember, tell them what you are going to tell them... then tell them... then tell them what you told them!... and then tell them again. Let's talk about each of these actions.

Connect with People

Too often I see the mistake of people starting a conversation with a stranger and "verbally throwing up on them." They immediately start out with a sales pitch to try and get someone to come and look at their opportunity. This is the absolute worst way to go about connecting with someone. When meeting an individual, get to know them first. Ask some questions about that individual and be sincere when asking them, and then pay attention to the answers they give you. Your objective is to connect with this individual and find out information about them. Not every person is going to be right for your opportunity, and by connecting with individuals you're easily able to sort through people until you find the person you're looking for.

When you do find someone that would be great for your opportunity, you've already connected with them and established some sort of relationship, which allows you to much more easily approach them with what you have to offer.

You will require several lead generation sources. There are tons of them out there; you just have to get creative. We'll go into these lead sources a little later in the book. But for now, if you're not out there finding people to connect with, you're not going to make any money.

The magic number is three to seven lead generation sources. I consistently have twelve. This is because I go by the philosophy of one of the greatest basketball players, Dr. J: "I expect more of myself than anyone else could possibly expect." This is how you create your success in a shorter period of time—by doing more than is expected.

Always be looking for more people. This is your business. You don't start at eight in the morning and then quit at five in the afternoon. You are always watching, meeting, and integrating. When you go to the movies, talk to the people standing next to you in line. When you're at the gas station, say hello to the person filling up next to you; when you're at the post office dropping off a package, ask how the cashier's day is going. Some of the greatest people I've been able to connect with were the servers in a restaurant. They're typically very good at connecting with someone because they already work in the service industry. I've been able to add amazing members to my team by simply connecting with the person serving me my meal. You get the point—you are always on the lookout to find more people!

Tell the Story

Expose your prospects to your company through the Web site, online videos, audiocassettes, brochures, recruiting packages, live or recorded guest presentation calls, Webinars, etc. If your company does not have these, then create them! Don't wait for others to create **YOUR** success. That would be *your* job! No one cares more about your success than you do! When first making contact, use a scripted approach until you're comfortable and familiar enough to do it on your own.

This is the point in the game when you start the "interview process." Not everyone is ready for your enterprise, and that's okay. It's necessary for you to "sort" through these connecting interviews with powerful questions and develop the ability to "hear what the person is really saying." One very common obstacle I often hear is "I don't have the money to get started in your enterprise." Be aware that if someone truly understood the value of your company, they would find the money. It is your job to tell the story in the most compelling way to help a prospect see the value your opportunity has to offer.

Share the story of your enterprise and your own personal success story with as many people as possible. One key element to remember in this part of the process is that "facts tell, stories sell." Facts are numbers, and people easily check out when someone starts rattling off statistics. They're unable to relate to this. However, when you share a story, a prospect is much more able to emotionally connect with you and see the value and power in the opportunity you're sharing with them. Become familiar with some of the key players in your enterprise so that you're able to share their stories with potential prospects. I'm always sharing the story of several other people in my company when meeting with a prospect and if possible, I'll call one of those individuals on the phone to have them speak directly to my prospect.

I've included below some of the scripts that I've used over the years. All of these scripts are designed to do three things: compliment, create curiosity, and get a commitment. These are known as the three Cs of recruiting. When used properly, these three Cs allow you to contact friends and associates in a very unoffensive and nonthreatening way.

Your intent at this stage of the process is to get a commitment from your prospect to review the information you will provide or meet with you personally. If they will not commit to review the information within twenty-four to forty-eight hours, then move on to others who will. Make an appointment to follow up with that individual. When contacting individuals from advertising, follow the cold market scripts you have access to and move them through the recruiting process. Remember, you are sorting, not selling. Don't chase people, just sort through them.

You'll want to use a warm market script when contacting your family, friends, and associates. There are three different methods in doing this; they include the front door approach, side door approach, and back door approach.

Here are examples of these different approaches:

Front Door Approach

Use this approach when contacting a prospect who perceives you as equally or more successful than they are. This is someone who has a level of respect or friendly feeling toward you.

Keep in mind that they will usually ask the question, "What's this all about?" Don't give them too much information. Let the system do the telling and selling. Invite them to investigate your business through the system and then plug them in. The real key to success is to say less to more people.

#1 Hey _____, if I could show you a way to make some serious cash fast, could you find time in your schedule in the next couple of days to take a look at it?

#2 Hi, _____, I'm glad I got a hold of you. Listen, I've only got a moment. I'm running out the door, but let me ask you a question. A while ago you told me you hated your job. Were you serious or were you just kidding around? (John says he was serious) Great, I've got a way for you to get out of it. I can't talk about it now. Let's get together tomorrow. I'd like to run a business idea by you!

#3 Hello, _____, I'm glad I got a hold of you! Listen, I've only got a moment. I'm running out the door, but I have something I want to talk to you about. How soon could we get together?

#4 _____, a friend of mine is expanding her business and asked me to keep a lookout for sharp, aggressive individuals. I think you qualify. If you're interested, I will get you some information!

#5 Hello, _____, this is _____. How are you doing? Great! Hey, the reason for my call is this. I have found a way to make some killer income. All I need is about two minutes so I can give you a thumbnail sketch of what we are up to, and then you can tell me whether or not you have some interest. Does that work for you? Okay! Have you ever heard of a company called _____? You haven't? This company allows you to work from home and make great money!

Side Door Approach

Use this approach when you contact someone you perceive to be better, stronger, or more successful than you. In other words, use this when you are "recruiting up." The perception has nothing to do with reality, but it has a lot to do with them being receptive to your invitation. The basic philosophy with this approach is to play yourself down and play up their ego. Here are some examples.

#1 Hello, _____, this is___. Did I catch you at a good time? Great! Hey, the reason for my call is this. I like you, I trust you, and I value your opinion immensely... and I need a favor. I have found a company by the name of _____. Because you have a good head for business, I would like you to take a look at this company for me and simply offer your opinion. I have a (CD, brochure, fifteen-minute message, etc) for your review. If I (drop a tape by, conference you into a call, etc.), will you (look at, or listen to) it? Great!

#2 Hi, _____. How are you? The reason for my call is that I have been introduced to a business that I think has some potential to be lucrative. I decided that before I jump in with both feet, I ought to have someone with your business experience check it out and see if I'm making the right decision. ___, if I could get the information together, would you please evaluate it for me?

#3 Hi, _____. I have always had a lot of respect for you and the success you've had in business. I'm getting involved in a business that appears to have some really exiting potential. But before I become too involved with it, I would like your professional opinion. Would you please do that for me? (Yes.) I will gather the information today and get it to you (or I can dial you into a conference call right now).

Back Door Approach #1

This approach is used for people who are very successful or for those you're not sure are dissatisfied. It's basically a "Who do you know that would like to make a lot of money?" approach. It gives them the opportunity to say "What about me?" or to refer names of people they believe will be interested.

#1 _____, I'm working with a new company, and I'm looking for some people who are sharp and might be interested in a change. Do you know anyone who would fit that description?

#2 _____, I'm looking to expand my business in your area.... Do you know anyone that is entrepreneurial and would have what it takes to head up an area, someone who is interested in making some serious money?

#3 _____, my company is looking for some sharp people who are dissatisfied with what they're doing now and might be interested in making some serious money. Do you know anyone who is looking for a change?

Back Door Approach #2

If you're talking to a stranger, the natural question comes up: "What do you do for a living?" or "Where are you from?" Here's how to use the answer to that question as an approach.

"What do you do for a living?' (Answer) "I teach people how to succeed in owning a business of their own while working from home." (After this statement don't say a word. Let them ask you for more details.)

"Where are you from?" (Answer) "Really? I am expanding my business in that area as we speak. Who do you know in your area that's ambitious and not afraid of making a lot of money?"

As you can see with telling the story, you're basically continuing the natural process of a conversation. After you've connected with an individual or you're speaking to someone you've already established a relationship with, then you simply share the bare minimums of your opportunity. Give them enough information to peak their curiosity and get them to the next event, which brings me to the next step in the process.

Build for Events

You'll want to build for events, whether it's a one-on-one, a two-on-one, or a house meeting, hotel presentation, Webinar, live guest presentation, or conference call, etc.

By now your guests' interest should be peaked. Regardless of the type of event you choose, you should physically take them to the event if at all possible. If it's a meeting and you know your guests, pick them up. If it's a conference call, then three-way them onto the call. Two of the best tools you have in this business are a pair of handcuffs and an automobile! I personally have never had a guest that I arranged to pick up not make it to the meeting. That's a clue. And after the event, make sure that your guests understand the concept of team building and how they get paid!

CRACKING the PRODUCERS CODE

When you're calling prospects and building for events, this is a great time to enlist your mentor's assistance. Give your mentor a brief background on your guest, especially details about the exposure they have had to your company. Call your guest and introduce your mentor. Here is how the call might go: "Hi, John, this is Chuck. As scheduled, I am calling you back. I know you may have a number of questions, so I took the liberty of inviting my mentor to be on the line with us. Chad has been very successful in this business and understands it well. John, let me introduce you to Chad. Chad, this is John."

Now, shut up! Don't say a thing, and especially don't interrupt, because that would not edify your mentor. You just sit, listen, and learn.

Let your mentor do his or her job. When I started I didn't have a story, but my mentor did, so I told his story while I worked on my own results. Even now when I make great money in my business, I still get my team in front of other people that are succeeding in the business, because my prospect will believe other people over me since I have something to gain by them buying my product.

Your mentor will share a personal story of success, answer questions, assess your prospect's level of interest, and build for the next event, if they qualify. The three-way call is designed to offer third party credibility, show the big picture, and assist your guest to make a decision. In the event that your mentor or upline is not available and you must make the call alone, do so with these objectives in mind. Find out if this is a "prospect" or a "suspect." If the person is a solid prospect, then build for the next event.

Every activity I do is with the intent of getting a prospect to the next event and then the next event after that and so forth until I've been able to establish a foundation with that person and get them dialed into the community side of my organization. When I have a prospect attends multiple events, especially in a short amount of time, then the success ratio of closing this individual increases substantially.

Events will drive your business! Get as many people to every single event you possibly can and then get them to the next event after that! This will be crucial to your business!

Follow Up

The final step in the recruiting process is following up with your prospect. Too many people go through all of the other steps and then lose steam during this last step. This is the close. Don't lose momentum! Your guest should be ready for a commitment by now. Ask, "Are you ready to start making money now?" or "Do you see any reason why you shouldn't get started?" Explain in detail the company package and make sure that you have answered every question that they might possibly have. At this point sign 'em up! If not, move on. Do not waste your time with uncommitted people.

By moving your guest from one exposure to the next, over time you'll become better and better at this process. Successful recruiting is all about the number of people you can get through the process and the time invested in assisting them to great success! You will always go much farther if it's not about the money! Your objective is to connect with people, tell the story (this means you must learn to give the presentation on your own), build for events, and follow up.

NOTES

6

Creating Your Contact List

Warm Market

Next on the list is to create a contact list and to start implementing different lead generation scenarios. Creating your contact list is a great way to implement the first recruiting step: *connect with people.*

The book *Acres of Diamonds* by Russell H. Conwell tells the story of Ali Hafed, an ancient Persian farmer. He left his farm and homeland in search of diamonds and great riches. After years of toil and sacrifice, he found himself penniless and distraught. In frustration, he took his own life. Later, one of the largest diamond discoveries of its time was made on Ali Hafed's farm. This story illustrates an important point. Many new associates leave behind acres of diamonds (their warm market) to go in search of sales elsewhere. They go to great lengths to avoid the very thing that will bring the fastest and greatest success. If you want to start fast, do the following: make a list of everyone that you know and then contact them! Every successful businessperson I know believes in referral marketing.

This can only happen by networking with friends, family, and business associates. You might cringe at the thought of contacting people you know about your opportunity. My advice is: Get over it! I've been in the game of networking all of my life and my contacts have made me a fortune. Why do you think people pay hundreds of thousands of dollars to join a country club? It's certainly not because the round of golf is that much better or the food is so exceptional. It's because of the networking and business opportunities that materialize from hanging out in those environments.

Networking your contacts for mutual benefit is no different in your enterprise than with any other business. One observation I've made of network marketers is that those who get out of the gate the fastest are those that have a strong network to tap into. This is because people do business with those they like and trust. If a person doesn't like and trust you, they're not going to do business with you. Just about everyone knows friends and associates that respect them for one reason or another. Friends will listen to them out of respect when a great moneymaking idea or business is presented.

This is what is commonly referred to as influence. Influence is what encourages many people to take their first look at an opportunity. Credible people with influence will cause your business to explode, because they're going to bring more people to the table than a marketer that doesn't have any leads.

Unlike the cold market, there's no relationship gap to bridge. I'm always looking for strong, credible, influential people, and I know they can lead me to contacts that I would have never met on my own. Those quality contacts generally don't require a lot of handholding. You can just get out of their way and watch them build. Another huge benefit of building your business through your network is that it doesn't cost you anything. And when you are first building your new business, you have to protect your financial resources.

Memory Joggers

Make a list of everyone that you know, even if it's only a first name. Use memory joggers, church lists, yearbooks, yellow pages, neighborhood lists, etc. The mind works by association. If someone asks you, "Who do you know?" you may pause for a moment and come up blank. But if someone asks, "Who do you know that is a doctor, a teacher, an aerobics instructor, a homemaker, a construction worker, etc., people immediately will probably come to mind. That's why you've got to open the phone book and just browse through the lists of various occupations. Open your professional directory and write down everyone you can think of.

Don't prejudge anyone, or you'll find out the hard way that if you don't approach someone, somebody else will. So, do you want them in your business, or should they just get started elsewhere? It's really up to you. Sooner or later, somebody is going to talk to them about your amazing opportunity.

Here are some memory joggers. Go through this list and write down every person you know with these occupations:

Accountant: CPA	Equipment: Office Machines, Copiers	Massage Therapist
Acupuncture	Events	Mechanical Contractor
Asst. Living: Home Care	Eye Care	Media: Radio Advertising
Advertising	Facilities: Meeting	Medical
Animals: Pet Boarding & Grooming	Financial Planner	Mortgage Lender
Appearance: Manicure/ Pedicures	Fitness: Personal Trainer	Moving & Storage
Appliances	Floors: Sales, Installation	Nutrition
Architect	Florist	Office Supply Company
Artist	Floral Design	Painting
Attorney: Business	Food: Personal Chef	Pest Control
Attorney: Divorce, Family Law	Funeral Home: Director of Planning	Pharmacy
Auctioneer	Furniture	Photography
Automotive Sales	Galleries	Physical Therapist
Automotive Services	Games & Supplies Dealers	Picture Framing
Banker	Garage Builders	Plumber
Billing Services	Garage Cabinets & Organizers	Pools: Sales & Service
Bookkeeping	Garage Doors & Openers	Printing
Business: Mail Boxes, Packing, Shipping	Garbage Disposal Dealers	Private Investigator
Carpet:Sales & Installation	Garden & Lawn Equipment Supplies	Public Relations
Carpet: Cleaner	Garden & Lawn Furnishings	Real Estate: Residential
Caterer	Gas Companies	Real Estate: Commercial
Chiropractor	Glass Companies	Real Estate: Appraiser
Cleaning: Maid Service	Golf Instructors	Records Management
Clothing Sales	Gardens: Center (Shop)	Scanning Service & Paper Shredding

CRACKING the PRODUCERS CODE

Coaching

Coffee Service

Collection Agency

Computer Sales & Service

Computer Software

Concierge

Construction: General Contractor

Cosmetics

Courier

Counseling

Credit Card Processing

Credit Union

Dentist

Dentist: Orthodontist

Direct Mail

Doctor

Dry Cleaner

Education: Language, Speech, etc.

Electrician

Electronic Home Systems Sales

Employment Staffing

Engineer

Entertainment: DJ

Environment: Bottled Water

Gift Baskets

Gifts: Balloons & Cakes

Glass: Stained Sales, Service

Graphic Design

Hair Salon, Nails

Health & Wellness

Health Spa / Day Spa

Heating / Air Conditioning

Image Consultant

Information Technology

Insurance: P & C

Insurance: Commercial

Insurance: Life, Health, Disability

Insurance: Long Term Care

Interior Design

Internet Service Provider

Janitorial

Jeweler

Landscaping

Loans: Commercial Loans

Lodging

Magazine

Marketing Consultant

Marketing: Email, Website

Renovation: Remodeling

Renovation: Woodwork

Renovation: Service/Repair

Roofing

Secretarial Service

Security Systems

Self-Defense

Signs

Telecommunications

Cabling Contractor

Local / Long Distance

Telephone Systems

Title & Escrow Agency

Training

Travel Agent

Tree Service

Veterinarian

Video & Sound

Videographer

Wedding Consultant

Windows: Blinds, Shades, Shutters

Wireless / Cellular

Top Twenty-Five

Once you've got everyone listed on a piece of paper, identify your top twenty-five prospects. Here are a few questions to assist you in identifying these top twenty-five people.

- Is this individual dissatisfied but successful?
- Is this individual a risk-taker?
- Does this individual have an entrepreneurial background?
- Does this person have any direct sales or network marketing experience?
- Is this individual a self-starter?
- Does this individual seem to have a high level of credibility with friends and associates? In other words, do they have influence?
- What is their work ethic?
- What is their past and current employment situation?

Identify these top twenty-five individuals as the people you would most like to be in business with.

You'll want to make a great first impression on these individuals when introducing your enterprise, so it will be very important to enlist the assistance of your mentor to contact and follow up with your top twenty-five list.

Building these contact lists will give you a confidence that you would otherwise lack. If you build a solid list of a couple hundred people, your attitude is going to be one of abundance. You don't ever want to be in a position of lead poverty consciousness. That will take you out of the business. Instead, make your list and continue to add to it daily so that your list is always full of untapped opportunity. By doing this, before you know it your database will be filled with thousands of people.

NOTES

_____

_____

_____

_____

_____

_____

_____

_____

_____

_____

_____

_____

_____

_____

_____

_____

Warm Market

In the last chapter, we touched on how to go about creating your contact list and the different methods to go about creating that list. We talked about the importance of your warm market and how when an individual taps into that their levels of success increases tremendously. My personal mentor utilizes only his warm market and the three-foot rule when marketing. He has become so good at sharing his opportunity with everyone he meets in an unassuming kind way that his closing ratio is something that deserves a book on its own.

Three-Foot Rule

Let's talk about the importance of the three-foot rule. Never underestimate its power! This means that you speak to people everywhere you go. This is one of the best ways to gain someone's confidence because it is much easier to establish trust and confidence one-on-one than over the phone. I speak to people everywhere I go. I speak to the person sitting next to me on the airplane. I speak to the person standing next to me in line at the supermarket, or when I'm filling up my car with gas. I don't start out with the idea of getting someone to sign up for my company, however. I legitimately want to meet and learn about them. We start to have a conversation and eventually they always ask what I do for a living.

When you're first talking to someone, you're able to ask qualifying questions and find out if this is an individual you'd want to collaborate with. You can determine if this is the opportunity that they may have been looking for and how serious they are at creating change in their life.

Whenever you frequent public places—malls, movie theaters, coffee shops, garage sales—wherever you go, you have an opportunity to connect with someone. Don't start a conversation with the anticipation of selling a product. Talk to them about who won the game last night or the huge snowstorm last weekend. But be

prepared, because when the opportunity arrives you must know what to say and how to say it. Don't freeze when they ask you what you do for a living, and don't jump into a sales pitch. That will close down the conversation quickly; the person won't be able to get away from you fast enough. Approach conversations like this with an attitude that this is a really nice person you would like to get to know better, and they'll feel that sincerity. Trust me, the opportunity will come for you to share with them information about your enterprise.

Some of my very best prospects have come from the three-foot rule. I'll never forget the time I was in the grocery store, standing in line to check out and speaking on my cell phone to a potential prospect. The woman standing in front of me could overhear my conversation. As she was getting ready to leave, she leaned over the person with me, handed me her business card, and asked if I would please call her. She wanted to get some more information about what I did for a living.

Networking

Networking is an art. If you're going to build your business, you require teammates. You want to attract all types of people, but you especially want to attract centers of influence. Don't prejudge people—"every dud knows a stud." When you attract individuals with large spheres of influence, your business is propelled forward at a much faster rate. You're looking for the players versus the pretenders. Look for good people who are going to lead you to more good people. The people who perceive themselves to be too busy are exactly the people I'm looking for. I'd rather have someone who is too busy and works their enterprise only part-time than someone who has lots of time and is a couch potato.

There are different ways of networking. Someone might be a great catch, but they're not interested in a career change… but they know people. Find a reason to exchange business cards and let them know you may be able to assist them with their business. Let them know that you'd like to sit down with them and show them how they could earn money for simply sending referrals your way. Money talks—it's all about what's in it for them. The movers and shakers are the people who make things happen.

Your objective is to find people who can open up their rolodex and call twenty key heavy-hitters that they personally have relationships with.

Do business with people you already do business with. Find *your* center of influence. Look for the movers and shakers. Go to local clubs and develop the relationships with these people. These are the "big fish." It takes time to develop these relationships and create trust. If you can develop relationships with these big fish, they'll be able to introduce you into their circle of influence, and more doors will continue to open. You could land speaking engagements at their organization's meetings. What an opportunity it would be for you to be chosen to represent your enterprise in front of an influential organization! So it boils down to you.... Are you the type of person that a center of influence would trust their circle of influence with? Do you look good? Do you speak well? What are your actions like? Are you respectful? Do you have a hungry salesman mentality, or do you have a genuine sincerity to assist others?

If you approach any of these organizations looking to grab whatever you can, they'll quickly push you away. Organizations are looking for individuals who are there to serve. Get involved with your local chamber of commerce. They're always looking for people who can promote the community through their businesses. Chambers of Commerce host breakfasts, lunches, and mixers for this purpose.

There's no excuse for not having people to talk to. Get involved in a little league, a bowling team, or an investment association, but get involved with the intention to serve, because the law of reciprocity teaches that you get what you give. Go into these networking atmospheres with a sincere intention to serve, and you'll be rewarded with much more than you ever gave. Like Napoleon Hill says, "The harvest will come with such force that you will wonder where it has been your entire life."

You can work with church groups, even if they have a "no sales" policy. If you develop relationships, then the cream will rise to the top and they'll to you. There isn't any rule that says you can't do business after the fact. You can also do this with the Boys and Girls Clubs. Those who educate dominate in a community.

The more money I make, the less focused I am on any "need" to make money, and the more people want to give me their money. Try to put yourself into areas and situations with high caliber people. For example, when I fly, I always fly first class. This isn't because I'm too good to sit in coach, but because the players sit in first class. I always try to get there as early as possible so I can sit in my comfy first class seat and pull out my prospecting list and begin making phone calls—the walls have ears, and I want everyone in that entire section to overhear me prospecting. Almost every time I do this, someone signs up in my enterprise.

Never verbally throw up on people. You don't want to come on too strong or too fast; instead you want to be coy and put yourself in situations where sharp individuals ask you what you do. I like to be dumb as a fox and set up situations where people can overhear me so that the curious ones that have an interest will approach me. When they approached me, they have just given me permission to prospect them.

If you have the intention of attracting high caliber people, there is a catch: You have to be a high caliber person yourself. Decide who you are in advance. A few days ago I was in a Subway, eating a tasty turkey sandwich. I took the opportunity to prospect while I was eating by making calls on my cell phone. There was a gentleman sitting with his son two tables away from me who could overhear my conversations, and as I got up to leave I knew he was going to ask me what I did for a living. This gentleman came to one of my group presentations the next day.

Another phenomenal example: I was in line at a sporting goods store, talking to a gentleman in Florida about the benefits of my enterprise, when the lady in front of me who overheard my conversation asked me for a business card. I gave her my card and also asked for her name and number. I brought her to my very next meeting and she joined my venture. Your business shouldn't be something that you only work nine to five. If you interweave your business into your daily activities, you'll pick up additional leads along the way.

It's very important to have credibility in your marketplace. There are so many factors that play into this. Your attitude, your appearance, your actions, how you carry yourself, your experiences, your mannerisms—all of these impact your credibility. How would you rate your credibility? You only attract people at the level of your credibility. However, you can control this. You can develop a higher level of credibility and begin to attract different individuals.

I'm at the top of my game now, but there was a time when I worked at my father's dry cleaners. If I can do it, so can you. I invested in myself and in my education. Because of this, I've been able to increase my level of influence. Come to the table with confidence. Know that you're representing one of the best brands on the marketplace.

When I was in the dry cleaning arena, I didn't have any credibility because I wasn't an entrepreneur. I didn't have a lot of respect, but when I decided (the Latin root of "decide" is "to cut off from") that I was going to be someone different, I thought to myself, *If I was successful, how would I walk? How would I talk? How would I think? How would I dress? What would I do?* I started doing those things in advance, and ultimately I became that person. I went out and bought a briefcase, a cell phone, and business cards before I was even a part of anything.

Warm Market

Your warm market is your most critical lead generation source. Approaching your warm market is one of the best and also one of the scariest scenarios. There is a way to do it in a nonthreatening way, however.

Typically you'll contact somebody, let them know you've found a new opportunity, and ask them if they know of anyone who might be interested. They'll usually say, "Well... me!" If they like you and trust you, they'll get started with you. If they don't, then they won't. Why not start with people you already know and have established trust with versus concentrating so much of your efforts in the cold market?

The more influence you have, the more you'll be able to persuade people to get started with your business. Make a list and build it wide and deep. Write down every single person you know and then go about making that initial contact. If you don't contact your warm list, someone else will. I've actually had people I know show up to a presentation at my home who were approached by someone else. Ouch! When it comes to contacting friends and family, if you're not willing to contact them, you're not really committed to your business.

Give them a call to let them know that you've come across a company they might be interested in. Give them the name of your company and let them know that this is an amazing opportunity that assists people to [insert what your company does here]. Tell them some success stories of individuals in your company. Tell them that the reason you're calling is that you would like to be in business with them, and you'd like for them check this out because of the wealth that the two of you could create together. Then, when they commit, let them know that you will pick them up (if it's a meeting) or schedule a one-on-one appointment to meet with them directly.

Your opportunity is like a pile of gold bars on the side of the road. Let's say that you get a flat tire on your car. You change the tire and as you lay the tire iron down on the side of the road, you hear a "clink." You look down and see a bar of gold sitting there. You pick it up and there are two bars under it; you pick up those two, and there are four more bars after that. You fill your entire car up with gold bars. Would you call your friends and family and say, "If you've got the time, could you maybe drop by to help me get all of this gold?" or are you going to call your friends and family and tell them, "We're rich! Stop what you're doing, get down here now with a big truck and fourteen people. I'll explain when you get here!" If you approach people with that level of enthusiasm, they'll take you more seriously, and you'll get more results with less effort because enthusiasm is contagious. Enthusiasm is one disease you want to get!

How to Contact Your Warm Market

When contacting your warm market, you'll want to take a slightly different approach. Remember to keep the urgency and proper posture with them. Many people are too nervous or self-conscious to contact individuals in their warm market, so they keep putting it off when these really are some of the easiest people to contact. You've already established that connection and relationship, so the conversation is going to be much easier. Below are some outlines to assist you with this process.

How to Invite Friends, Family, and Business Associates to Take a Look at Your Business

(Your interview should be conversational. Rehearse this until you can make it flow naturally. Build a relationship with the person, but avoid too much idle chitchat. Stick to your purpose and maintain control of the conversation.)

Hello _____, this is _____. How are you doing? Glad to hear it. Have you got a few minutes to talk right now? Wonderful! The reason for my call is that I have found an opportunity to make money in (your business enterprise here) and I want to run it by you to see if you have some interest. Have you ever heard of a company by the name of *[your company name here]*?

(On the off chance that they have, you can say "I'm not surprised—what have you heard?" This will give you an opportunity to validate the company or overcome any objections and set an appointment. Of course, 99.9 percent of the time they will say they have not heard about your opportunity, and then just proceed with the interview as directed.)

Let me tell you about it. *[Let them know what your company specifically does.]* They are arguably the best in the country at what they do. Here is what this means to you: They are looking for people to get the word out and find customers, but they don't operate like most typical companies. You see, in our enterprise they don't hire their marketers as employees; instead, they bring them on as independent business owners that work with them to sell our product. This keeps overhead down and shifts most of the profit to their marketers. It allows you to work from home, set your own hours, work part-time or full-time, and enjoy all of the tax breaks that go along with owning your own business.

Let me just share a story or two about some of the people I get to work with, and how this business has impacted their lives. *[Share a few success stories about people in your company]*

The upside is huge, and the bottom line is that if anything I have said interests you, then we should meet... shouldn't we?

(Book the appointment and be sure to reconfirm within twenty-four hours of the meeting. Follow the dialog listed below to set the appointment.)

What works better for you, daytime or evening? Evening.... What evening is best—Tuesday or Thursday? Okay, I can make Thursday work. How about _____pm? Great, I'm driving to a company presentation where all the details will be explained. I'll come by and pick you up so we can ride together. Can you be ready at_____? See you then.

Contacting Friends

Hi, _____, this is _____. How's it going? Great! Do you have a couple minutes right now? The reason for my call is this: I am working with a handful of marketing geniuses. These guys have developed a marketing strategy that is creating huge success for its participants. I can't get into all of the details now, but I know people that have made $10,000-$20,000 for just inviting people to attend. I want you to come with me and see what all the excitement is about.

Contacting Your Top Twenty-Five List

When it comes to approaching the top twenty-five individuals on your warm list, involve your mentor. These are individuals that you look up to. You may feel as though you're not on an equal footing with them or maybe you haven't yet achieved their level of success. So you want to put a big fish on the phone with a big fish.

Start by edifying your mentor. Let the person know that you told your mentor about them and your mentor really wanted to meet them, so you hope it's okay, but you've got your mentor on the phone; ask if it would be okay for you to introduce them. At this point, sit back and be quiet. Let your mentor take over. He or she will protect your relationship with your friend. It is extremely important to not interrupt or de-edify your mentor. This is a great opportunity to contact people you would most likely never contact on your own.

NOTES

_____

_____

_____

_____

_____

_____

_____

_____

_____

_____

_____

_____

_____

_____

_____

_____

_____

Continuing the Journey

Continue on the Path of Self-Development

I can't stress enough the importance of personal improvement. I started out the book going over this, and I want to stop and take a moment to remind you of the importance of it again. You'll want to read, listen to, and hang around with positive, uplifting influences. Be sure to immerse yourself in personal development programs and make them a daily part of your schedule. Again, if you haven't already purchased *Think and Grow Rich* by Napoleon Hill, then you need to put down this book and go and purchase it right now.

It will be necessary for you to start to create a personal development library of your own. When you're trying to get to know someone, take a look at that person's library. What are they reading? What do they like to listen to? Who do they allow to speak to their minds, and what effects will materialize from that influence? This is your chance to better influence other people's lives. Introduce them to great books and audio series. By you consistently continuing on your own personal path of self-development you'll be better able to assist others with their own journey.

Become aware of what *your* library says about *you*. Is it full of *People* magazines or *Field and Stream,* or do you own books like *Think and Grow Rich* by Napoleon Hill? I've found that the best leaders were once the best students. Your library is a direct reflection of what matters most in your life.

Set Target Dates

Set target dates for your path to the top of your company. You can't make much money until you are reach the first level of leadership, so make sure that you completely understand your company's compensation plan and then put into

practice a plan to complete this process. The faster you reach leadership levels, the faster you become profitable.

After you've reached your first level of leadership, go over your business plan and goals again and set new ones, or adjust them to assist you with getting to that next level. You'll want to be consistent in this exercise and keep these models along with your target dates in a prominent place so that you're always reading them and keeping yourself familiar with them.

Develop Your Testimony

Visibility in our enterprise is priceless. Your testimony should be your own one-minute commercial about your business. You will want to keep it short and sweet and to the point. People have a short attention span—why do you think commercials are only thirty seconds long? Your testimony should include the following: product benefits you have experienced and the income opportunity and lifestyle changes you have enjoyed. It should be spoken naturally (not read from a script), and remember it should not be longer than one minute! Napoleon Hill always said, "...know what you wish to say, say it with all of the emotion you can, and then sit down!" Creating a story worth bringing you up to the front of the room will make you a fortune! If you are not being asked to share at every meeting, call, Webinar, or company event, then you are leaving money on the table. If your guests see you being edified in front of the room, they will automatically want to join you because of your leadership!

Fake It Until You Make It

I freakin' HATE that phrase! "Fake it until you make it" in my mind says... "Lie to people to get ahead." This is not cool. There is something very wrong about that! How in the world do you intend to have a profitable business that starts with a lie? No long-term success can happen under a false beginning. Try this instead: **DECIDE!** Decide who you want to be in advance! WOW! What a concept! Think about it. If you ran your business and your life like that, you could create your own script on life and business. If you walk, talk, and act like the person you want to become, the end result will be that you become the perfect you!

It comes back to that "have, do, be" mentality. People think that if they *had* a million dollars, they would *do* those things that millionaires do, and then they would truly *be* happy. This isn't a sincere way of living, and it's not being honest with oneself. I suggest you turn this around and develop a "be, do, have" mentality. If you'll *be* the person you want to become, then you'll *do* what that person would do, and you'll *have* everything in life that you could possibly want.

You must emulate the correct persona, because this concept can work in the negative as easily as in the positive! What you think about, you bring about! It is very important to decide up front the kind of person you want to become and know why. There is a price to be paid in every situation. Trust me—your friends, family, and maybe even your spouse will give you a hard time about *"deciding who you are in advance."*

You'll have to decide: Is the squeeze worth the juice? In other words, are you willing to stay the course? Will you pay to play? Do you have the guts to prove them wrong? The Latin root of the word "decide" is "to cut off from." So you must cut yourself off from any possibility of allowing anyone to take you off course. I have seen people that had so much potential it was scary, but they never got anywhere because they were afraid of what someone else would say. Take back your power and take control of the only thing you have complete control over—your mindset. *Decide who you are in advance!*

Continue to Be a Student of Your Business

Your education will never be complete. Success in life and business requires an eternal round of continuing education. Always remain teachable and coachable so you can adapt quickly to the constant changes you will be faced with.

One of the biggest reasons I've been able to achieve the level of success I have is because I realize that I have so much to learn, and I am willing to put my pride aside so that I will be open to receiving new information and lessons in life which in turn are invaluable to the thriving success of my business. It's imperative to always continue to learn more about your business, selling, communicating,

connecting, closing, and so on. There is so much information in this world to assist you with the success of your business. You just have to be open to receive it!

The only constant in life is change. Too many individuals fear change. Learn to embrace it and teach others to do the same. We are all both teachers *and* students! If you are always resisting change then eventually you will get left in the dust in this ever-changing world. Look at today compared to twenty years ago. People would have laughed at you if you'd told them about the Internet and digital cameras and the cell phone capabilities that we now have. Imagine where we're all going to be twenty years from today. Change is going to happen—it's up to you whether or not you're going to keep up with it or get left behind.

Develop Proper Posture

I could write volumes on this subject. Posture is not something you are born with. It is an attitude that you develop over time, a confidence that you gain through multiple victories, and a quiet intensity that you carry with you everywhere you go. It does not mean that you are rude or offensive, but rather that you have purpose and direction. Your time is precious, and your desire to succeed creates a sense of urgency that transmits to others around you. With posture come the memories of past successes and the expectation of future victories. Posture attracts others to you and drives your business, but it comes with a price. To develop it, you must become an avid student who is constantly committed to your own personal development—someone with self-discipline who reads positive books, listens to self-empowering audios, and attends life-changing seminars.

Posture has to do with the vibration level you currently operate from. What I mean is the energy you're emitting when connecting with an individual. For example, have you ever walked into a room and immediately noticed a particular person. This can be both for the good or the bad. We've all heard it, "That person has horrible energy." You may not even know this person and you haven't said a single word to them; however, you sense that they're in a bad mood or have an angry demeanor, and you don't have any desire to even say hello.

It can also work in the opposite direction; you can see a person and before even saying hello to them, you feel an instant positive energy being emitted from them. You are attracted to them and feel at ease being around them.

Think of the energy and vibration level that comes from very successful, high-powered individuals. Have you ever spent time around a prominent political figure or the CEO of a company? You may find yourself in awe of this person and have the desire to learn more about them.

I've been working on my posture and the energy I emit since the age of nineteen when I first read *Think and Grow Rich* by Napoleon Hill. I'm still working on it and will continue to do so until I die. Recently, I was eating dinner at a restaurant with a group of individuals. The manager of the restaurant walked up to me and asked me if a certain vehicle out in the parking lot belonged to me. My vehicle has advertising on it for my enterprise. Everyone at that table was admonished that the manager walked directly up to me to ask me if that was my car. The manager didn't see me get out of my car, yet he automatically knew that I was the driver of this vehicle. He then began to ask me questions about my enterprise and what I did for a living. Wouldn't you love for situations like that to happen?

There is a reason why Napoleon Hill was commissioned by Andrew Carnegie to study 500 of the richest and most successful individuals during their lifetime. A large part of this was to determine their posture and the energy that they emitted. Through the association of like-minded individuals, you will develop posture and with it success. Posture also requires that you let go of people in your life that hold you down! We give way too much power to individuals in our lives that have no success! So, don't take advice from someone who is more broke than you. Grab the coattails of someone who gets it, and carbon copy them!

Create Urgency

The idea of creating urgency is so important. One of the most successful and popular resources you have is your company's weekly meeting. Remember, your time is valuable, so it is extremely important to create urgency about attending these events for those in your organization. Your desire to succeed also creates a sense of urgency that is transmitted to others around you.

For example, my company held a meeting every Thursday night, and my mentor was always at that meeting. But when I would prospect, I would say, "You're in luck, because this Thursday night, my mentor Bob will be at this presentation. Please remind me to introduce you to him." Again, Bob was always at this meeting, but the prospect doesn't have to know that. All they have to know is that he is going to be at the meeting that's coming up. A sense of urgency is one of the most important tools you have, because unfortunately, people are lazy and if they know that they have the chance to come anytime, they'll keep putting it off and say they'll come next week.

NOTES

Become a Master

Master Five Areas

There are five critical characteristics that I have found to be character-building blocks on which I've built myself and my business. They are virtues that we are all taught about from the moment we are born and will continue to hear about for the rest of our lives. These are virtues that apply to everything in life, and I feel it necessary to touch on them in this book. They are:

- Desire
- Commitment
- Integrity
- Loyalty
- Work

Desire

The one thing that has kept me moving past the adversities in my life has been my desire to succeed. I have developed a deep, burning desire to succeed, and I will not let anyone or anything take that away from me. This is what gets me out of bed in the morning and propels me through the day. It is because of this burning desire that I'm able to remain consistent in my productive activities and take my work and what I'm doing seriously. It is because of my desire that I begin every morning with the phrase, "I get to, I want to, I choose to"!

Your desire is a reflection of your why that we discussed at the beginning of the book. If your why isn't big enough, then your desire will fizzle out early in the game and you won't have the gumption to stay in the game long enough to achieve any real success.

I challenge you to reconnect with your why every single day—multiple times in a day, if necessary—to assist you in keeping that burning desire alive inside of you!

Commitment

This is just doing what you said you would do. It's that simple.

Integrity

Integrity is a characteristic born within and developed into an outward expression of who you are and the principals you adhere to. Your actions reveal your integrity more clearly than your words do. Your gives comfort to those who trust you to do what is right above what is profitable.

Integrity is one of the most important virtues that you will ever have in your business. It is how honest you are in your dealings with yourself and with others. Once you have compromised your integrity with someone, it can sometimes be impossible to get back. No matter what you do in your business, do not ever compromise your integrity! I will not do business with someone who doesn't have integrity. Period.

Loyalty

Loyalty, just like respect, must be earned and is given over time to those who have shown it in return. Loyalty requires sacrifice; maybe it means sticking by a friend when nobody else will. It is a quality characterized by discipline. It requires simple daily acts that if repeated over time lead to victory. It calls for stability and even-mindedness, and those that possess it are a lot like the tortoise that, in spite of limitations, still comes out a winner!

I have gone out of my way numerous times for individuals who may have been struggling on my team and required additional support because of their loyalty to me and our enterprise. However, if someone is struggling, and they're also a fence-sitter or always looking for a better deal, than I am not quite as willing to invest the same amount of time with them.

Work

To many people, work is a four-letter word. To me, it's a three-letter word: FUN! So many people have said to me, "Man, you're lucky!" Nothing annoys me more when people say that, because luck happens when preparation, hard work, and timing all match up. Oftentimes when I'm working, I will play games with myself to keep it fun.

I used to imagine that the CEO of my company and my upline leader had a crystal ball and could see everything I was doing or not doing in my business. I imagined that they would be handing out opportunities in the future, and whether or not I received those opportunities would be based upon what they saw of my work ethic. Be willing to do what others are not willing to do, and you'll have what they'll never have. Tied in very tightly with your work ethic is your belief and the level of your expectation for success.

We attract what we think about on an ongoing basis. Napoleon Hill said, "Whatever the mind of man can see and believe it can achieve." Have you heard that one anywhere before? (By the way, have you picked up that book yet?) Success requires no explanations and failure allows no alibis. Work hard, believe in yourself, do things for the right reason, and everything will work out.

NOTES

Lead Generation

Treat Your Business Like a Business

Stay involved in moneymaking activities. Do not fall prey to the entrapment of busy work. Always remember, there are only four things that constitute moneymaking activities. Once again, they are connect with people, tell the story, build for events, and follow up. With this in mind, let's discuss some of the ways that you can generate those prospects to talk to.

Continue to Generate Leads

Successful associates always keep the pipeline full. If you're not dialing, you're dying. There is no such thing as a fence-sitter in this business. You are either progressing forward or falling back. Your appointment book will reveal the direction you've chosen. It's important to have three to seven lead sources! If you really want to succeed, develop seven to fourteen. It's time to get off of your ASSetts and get to work! Remember the story I told you earlier about the basketball player, "Dr. J"? He had higher expectations for himself than anyone else did, and I am the same. That is why I consistently have twelve different lead generation sources.

I can promise you that what most people do all day is not enough to become a top income earner. If you want to make a little money, then do a little work. If you want to make a ton of money, then don't be afraid to roll up your sleeves and get to work.

I have changed the word work from a four-letter word to a three-letter word: FUN! If it's fun, then it's not work... you could go all day and all night. Years ago when I worked at a dry cleaners, pressing clothes, I couldn't wait to call it a day and go do something "fun," but when you enjoy your work, it's not work! Now when

SIEGFRIED & ROY'S FIRST MARKETING CAMPAIGN

I'm making prospecting phone calls and connecting with individuals, I enjoy it. I'm getting to know a number of new people every single day and share an opportunity that could potentially change their life. That is fun! I love it! That is why I'm able to do it and continue to do it.

Lead Generation

We've already touched on your warm market, but you'll also want to have other lead sources sending potential prospects your way. You'll want to start advertising and generating leads from outside sources. Remember that toll-free number we spoke about earlier? Now is a great time to get that set up. When people call your phone number, if they like what they hear they'll leave their name and number, and you'll have the opportunity to call them back. But to get people to call you requires that you get out there and start generating the leads.

Flyers

The first lead source is flyers. This was my bread and butter when I first started in this industry. I would pass out flyers from the beginning of the evening until early the next morning. Passing out flyers is a numbers game. If you pass out 10,000, you may only get 100 calls.

This was the number one way I generated leads when I first started. Passing out flyers takes a fair amount of time, so there are a couple of ways to do this. You can pass them out yourself, or you can hire other people to do it for you. Flyers are a great way to get going in your business. If doesn't matter what color paper you use; however, I've found that yellow paper with black bold writing is the best.

There are a number of phrases you can put on your flyers, so I suggest that you use what motivates you. Here are some examples of flyers that I use (don't forget to add your telephone number to all of these):

- Fire Your Boss—Double Your Income! I Did!
- I Work at Home and Love It—You Can, Too!
- Make Excuses or Make Money, Not Both!

It doesn't matter so much what the message is; what matters is getting the flyers out there. Too much information on a flyer is ineffective, so keep it short and simple.

One of the key elements of passing out flyers is your mindset. When you're passing out flyers, you must be proud that you're passing out flyers. Your focus is on all the people you are going to assist.

Because of this, I've always received lots calls from my flyers. There were times when I would put out between 1,000 to 10,000 flyers a day. I used to go out at 4:00 in the morning to pass out flyers—winter, spring, summer, and fall. It was a great way to start the day. When passing out flyers, you'll want to go where there are a lot of vehicles, like apartment complexes. Make sure that your flyers aren't too big (maybe six to a page), and then print them on a nice stiff cardstock. Slip the flyer in the driver's side door in between the black rubber and the car's window. (Do not put it on the windshield.) You want to get your flyer noticed, and you want it to be convenient.

So much of this is about energy. You can walk into a room and tell the negative people from the positive people simply by the energy that they emit. A piece of your energy gets left with each flyer that you pass out. This is why your mindset and attitude is so important when passing out flyers. Your attitude applies to everything that you do in this business.

When you're passing out flyers, if a sign says "Do Not Pass Out Handbills," then don't do it. Because of this, mall parking lots are not the best place to go. If there isn't a sign posted, the general rule is that you can pass them out. However, check your local laws.

Flyers appeal to a lot of people because they're a low budget way to get your advertising out there. You've got to pass out hundreds and thousands of flyers consistently before you can expect results. I've had people who have had my flyer sitting in their car or purse for months before they called me.

Don't worry about saturating the market. I've had people who called after the tenth flyer because they decided they had to find out what it was all about. If you study advertising you'll find that agencies have one philosophy: market saturation. They know that, while there are a certain amount of individuals that will take action after seeing an ad once or twice, the general population will take action after seeing something five to ten times, and an even larger part of the population will take action after being exposed to something fifty to sixty times. The information has become engrained in them, they accept that the product is reputable, and they're now willing to take action. Repetition is the key when it comes to advertising and marketing. So, you'll probably hit the same condo and apartment complexes multiple times before getting results. When you're out shopping, hit the parking lots, pass out flyers at grocery stores, your local drugstore, the bookstore—wherever you go.

Business Cards

Instead of using flyers, lately I've been using business cards. Business cards serve several purposes. When people get them, they put them in their wallet or purse. When you're on a small budget, they're extremely effective because you can fit quite a few on a single page. It's also very easy to keep a large stack in your bag so that you have quick access to them whenever you pull into a parking lot. They're easier for you to handle, and technically they're not handbills. But again, check your local business laws. Remember when advertising, less is more. (I don't mean less advertising—I mean less information.)

Door Hangers and Sandbags

Two other types of flyers are door hangers and sandbags. I use door hangers in residential areas where I know there are probably a lot of housewives. Do not tape flyers to someone's door; make sure that they're attached to the doorknob. You can hit specific neighborhoods with door hangers.

You can make your own sandbags by filling a ziplock bag with a flyer and some silica sand. Silica does not retain any moisture, so it will keep your flyer dry. (Do not put rocks into these bags. If you do, you will get calls from people stating that you threw it through their window, etc.) You can have a lot of fun distributing sandbags with a partner, and you can throw out thousands in a single evening.

Just to give you a heads up, not everyone that calls your number is going to be positive. You have to become thick-skinned. Don't take offense. Everybody has an opinion, but don't waste your time with any negative energy. Move on to somebody who is looking for your opportunity.

One more piece of advice—if you're going to pay someone to do this, pay them a little bit up front, and then pay them according to results. They will be much more apt to actually pass them out. And remember, nothing works if you don't. As they say in advertising, "Everything works and nothing doesn't."

Handbills

Handbills are another great source of advertising. This is a flyer that you hand to someone directly. You can pass these out at concerts, sporting events, etc. It does require you to step out of your comfort zone, because you'll get rejected quite a bit. Don't take it personally, just move on to someone who is willing to take your information. If someone seems interested, make sure you get *their* name and phone number so you can follow up with them at a later time.

Another thing with handbills: People view adults passing things out a little differently then they view children. So, if you want to employ your children to pass out handbills, not only is it a tax write-off, but most people aren't going to say no to a kid. Kids will get three to four times more handbills passed out than adults. Handbills are a great way to overcome your fear of rejection. Remember, I would rather be rich than right. I'm willing to do whatever works for my business. Frank Sinatra said it best: "The best revenge is massive success."

Fish Bowls

A fish bowl is using an empty goldfish bowl as a vehicle to collect business cards. You may have developed a relationship with a local business owner. Ask them, "May I buy a lunch or give a gift certificate to one of your existing customers to get them to come back here again?" What are they going to say? You can easily set up a weekly free lunch drawing. All you require is a fishbowl and a little sign that says, "Enter to Win—Free Drawing." Everyone wins in this scenario—the customer thinks the business owner is giving away a free lunch, the business owner gets more business, and you win because at the end of each week you get all the business cards or entry forms that are left.

Billboards

This lead generation method is one that requires some cash up front. Billboards are all over the nation, and they do get results. A lot of time a billboard campaign is shared. If for example you have five people, you may want to set up a rotating number so that you have one number, and then every time someone calls it will switch according to who is next in line to get the call. You must have a strong headline on a billboard, and the phone number is critically important; it must be one that it is easily remembered. Billboards are expensive, so this is not the biggest bang for the buck when it comes to lead generation.

Bulletin Boards

There are two opportunities to generate leads with bulletin boards found in restaurants and business establishments. First, you can put up flyers and business cards. You can also reverse-market other individuals that advertise on these boards. A lot of them aren't making what they would like to be making.

When I first started and didn't have a lot of leads, I took cards and flyers from bulletin boards at schools and businesses, and then I called those people. Now, there is a specific technique to use with this form of cold calling. When I called them, I talked to them as if I already knew them. For example, I have Dave the plumber's business card. Well, I would picture Dave in my mind, and then I would call him and say, "Hi Dave, this is Chad. I was thinking about you today. I have this phenomenal opportunity that I think you would be very interested in." At this point, Dave is thinking, *Is this my sister's uncle's son?* Most of the time, the person doesn't even ask me who I am. This is because I am so confident in the conversation; I ask him if he's open to new opportunities, and then I give him the information. I've had people come to my meetings, decide to join my business, and then ask me, "Who are you?"

I tell them I just called them from their business card. "Dave" then tells me that I talked to him like I knew him. I tell him that yes, I speak to everyone as if I already know them.

This is a great way to get leads, and it doesn't cost you a dime. At any given time, I've got a stack two to three inches high of people to call, because I know that just like me, there are millions of people stuck in jobs they don't enjoy. I know that if someone had found my card and contacted me with an opportunity, I would have been in. There is no excuse for someone to experience lead source poverty.

I've even gotten my kids involved with this activity. I was recently eating at a local restaurant with my kids and my oldest daughter walked over to the bulletin board and pulled off a number of the business cards. She then wrote her initials in the upper corner of each card and gave them to me. This way, if any of those potential leads join my enterprise, she'll get a piece of any commission I receive. Talk about being a proud father!

T-Shirts, Books, Buttons, Etc.

T-shirts are another great way to generate new leads. My personal mentor knows someone that dresses their kids in a t-shirt that says, "If you don't make 20K, then you need to call my dad." It's a simple message, but it's got some meat to it. When you talk about graphics on a t-shirt, the simpler it is, the better. It's got to be legible, professional, and quickly get the message across.

As you're out and about on the bus or in the mall, carry a book like *Rich Dad Poor Dad*. People will be attracted to you because of this, and you'll be able to ask them, "Have you applied what you're learning in these books?" When they tell you no, a door has just been opened for you to share your business opportunity.

Find items that will attract attention to you. Wear a button that says, "Ask me how to make 20K a month." You don't have to be a social debutante. You just have to be willing to attract attention and share your opportunity in a credible fashion. Those who have "status" won't do scenarios like this; they don't want to attract attention to themselves because they have "status." This is hilarious to me, because the more money I get the more I'm willing to swallow my pride and get rid of any idea that I'm too good to do something, whether it's wearing a button, passing out flyers, or whatever else it takes to generate leads for my business.

Another great lead source is placing a flyer in a book in the real estate and personal development section of a bookstore. The people browsing in this section are typically interested in an opportunity already. I'm in bookstores all the time because of my personal desire to continually be progressing in my personal development and keeping abreast with what is going on in the marketplace. I want the same types of individuals in my enterprise. What better place to find them than in a bookstore? What better place to put my contact information than inside a book, just sitting there on the shelf waiting to be purchased?

What it all comes down to is being creative and thinking of ways to get noticed and to have people ask you about your business opportunity. If you can put yourself out there and force yourself into a situation where you're forced to respond, then you will start to overcome your fear of rejection.

Signs

Car signs, window signs, and car wraps are all great ways to generate leads as well. You can put vinyl magnets on the side and back of your vehicle. Be very careful, though; make sure you wash both the back of the magnet and the side of your car before placing the magnet, and then, every two to three days remove the magnet to avoid scratching the paint on your vehicle. You can also place vinyl lettering on the windows of your car. One time I took my family to California, and I had so many leads who called me by the time I got back that I had a hard time returning all the calls.

You can also ask someone you know if they'll let you put advertising on their car. Get a separate toll-free number so you can give them a portion of profits that come in from any calls you get.

Joint Ventures

Here's a story about joint ventures. A pharmacist was looking at expanding, and he came up with a brilliant idea one October. He wanted a very profitable December, so he approached a friend who owned a jewelry store and asked him, "If I could bring customers to you that you wouldn't have received otherwise, would you split the profits with me?" His friend said yes, so the pharmacist wrote a letter to all of his existing customers, thanking them for their loyalty. At the end of the letter he said that he wanted to do something more than just thank them; he offered them 15% off any jewelry purchased in his friend's store if they brought the letter in. This man generated an additional $73,000 in profit. Not bad!

I recently ran a joint venture with a local business owner. Here is an example of what the letter said:

Dear Valued Customer,

This letter is in appreciation for you choosing (insert your company business name here). We do our best to provide the highest quality service, and if there is anything we can do to serve you in the future, please let me know.

Instead of just saying thank you, I wanted to do something for you. I have come across a great opportunity that had has to do with (insert applicable information here). I've been able to develop a relationship with (insert joint venture partner name) and watch as this individual and others have created tremendous wealth because of their partnership with this company.

I am offering you the opportunity to participate in an event on (input a specific event or offer here).

Seating is limited, so those of you who are absolutely serious about changing the quality of your financial life, get back to me A.S.A.P. to reserve one of ten front row seats.

Sincerely,

XXXXXXXX

Newspaper Ads

Newspaper ads are a great lead source. In the beginning I ran a full-page ad, thinking that I could put all sorts of information in it. I spent $4000 dollars, and I got one phone call from a person who was trying to reverse-market me. I then decided to listen to my mentor who had originally told me to create a little classified ad for $37, and from this ad I got twenty-five phone calls. "If it ain't broke, don't fix it!" I had to learn the hard way.

I've always watched my local papers, because often there would be thirty to forty ads from my company, all with similar language. It's a good idea to see who else is in there, because an interested prospect going through the paper will call ten different ads to find the very best solution for them. So, if you notice too much competition in one paper, find another paper. Just make sure that your method of advertising is going to lead the crowd, not follow it. Most ads run for about three weeks, and this is when you can put your ad back in. Remember, less is more. Be bold and direct.

Where your ad is placed is very important as well. You want it in the Help Wanted section, *not* the Business Opportunity section. (The papers don't want you in the Help Wanted section, though.) I like to get my ads noticed, so I'm very specific with the newspapers about both the wording and the placement of my ads.

Online Ads

There are also many free online ad sources. One of the most popular is Craig's List; however, almost every national and local publication also has online ad sources. Some offer free classified ads online, and others charge a nominal fee. This is your chance to get to know your local community. Find the local city publications and newsletters that are published monthly and quarterly. Visit local community and government centers, as well as churches. Many of them publish newsletters or have bulletin boards where you can advertise. Check out local universities and colleges.

All higher education institutes have their own newspapers, and it is often very inexpensive to advertise in these papers. All of the different departments also have their own bulletin boards where you can advertise.

Purchasing Leads

You can also purchase leads from lead sources such as Cutting Edge Media. There are different price ranges to fit different budgets. Cutting Edge Media creates television commercials that attract people looking for home-based businesses; they screen the leads and then offer them for sale.

The downside is that many of these companies sell those leads to multiple people, so when you purchase leads, you'll want to contact them immediately. For example, I set time aside to call these people on Mondays. Yes, you'll still have people who hang up on you and get angry, or their information isn't exactly accurate. Just deal with it. People often blame the leads ("These leads suck!"), but more often than not, it's their prospecting skills that... well, suck. Becoming a master prospector requires developing your skills on the phone. You'll always encounter some bad leads, but reputable leads companies will let you test their leads in small amounts first.

Here is an example of what I say to someone when calling from a purchased lead source:

"Hello there, is _____ in? Hi, _____, this is Chad, and you don't know me. The reason for my call is, as I understand it—and please correct me if I am wrong—is that you were looking for a way to generate additional income while working from home. Is that still the case?"

IF NO: "So, let me clarify: you are not interested in making more money from home?"

IF YES: "Great, I just need a couple of minutes to ask you a few questions, and then I'll give you some info on our company. Is now a good time?"

"What do you do for a living?"

"How long have you done that?"

"It must be very satisfying!"

"What would you like to be doing?"

"Ideally, how much income would you like to make each year?"

"If I can show you a legitimate way to earn the money you want in the next twelve months, would that be worth it to you?"

Then, go on to tell them about your company and determine if it might be a good fit for them.

Resumes

If you're contacting someone off a resume, keep in mind that these individuals are searching for employment. Make sure that you don't lead them to think that this is an employment opportunity. It is an *income opportunity;* make it clear that they will be in business for themselves. As long as you're up front and honest when beginning a conversation with someone that came from a resume, you'll often find that they are interested in an income opportunity. There is a reason they put their resume online… they're searching for something better!

When I opened up a new market for my company, I found almost everyone through posted resumes. Since you are going to be contacting people directly, do your research and find good companies. (I've used Career Builder and Monster.) I invited each person to come to a group interview. I told them up front that I'd be setting them up as independent contractors, not employees, so that they would have tax benefits. Many of these people are looking for opportunities; you just have to assist them to adjust their thinking to being in business for themselves. I always advertise for sales and marketers, people who are familiar with working with people already. I'm looking for folks who will go out and bring business back, not people who sit back and wait for business to come to them.

When calling someone from a resume, here is an example of a script that I have used:

Resume Script

Hi, this is Chad. I got your resume from a recruiter who thought you might be a good fit for what I am working on based on your resume on Hotjobs.com. How are you? Great!

Do you have a couple of minutes to talk right now?

Do you mind if I ask you a few questions?

First off, what is making you look for a new opportunity?

What would you say is your greatest strength?

What would you say is your greatest weakness?

Did you post your resume because you are looking for supplemental income, or a total change in career?

Good! I believe we can help.

I represent a company called _____—we deal in (insert your company information here).

Are you familiar with this product?

If NO: Great! Let me give you some information about my enterprise and what we have to offer you if you're the candidate I'm currently looking for.

If YES: Great! Tell me what you already know about XXXX?

Let me tell you a little bit more about me and the company. As I mentioned, I represent XXXXX. We've established an opportunity for people to set themselves up as independent contractors so that they're able to work from home and have the opportunity to create phenomenal wealth.

When our founders created our company, they wanted to *really* create something where people like you and I would be given exactly what we require to become successful business owners.

Like you, I had no _____ (time, money, knowledge), and I was afraid of risking what I didn't have. When I met the people involved with this company, I knew it was a great opportunity for me to work with and show others how to create financial freedom.

Let me ask you this, if there were people to hold your hand, and you could be involved in a network of like-minded investors who could help walk you through the training process would you be interested?

Tell me, what would you be doing today if you didn't have to go to work?

Ideally, how much monthly income would you like to have coming in to quit your job?

Now, it won't happen overnight, but it can happen. Some of the people I work with have been able to quit their jobs in about three to six months.

I am looking for sharp people who are interested, motivated, and serious about making more money.

I'm not sure whether or not this is for you. I am trying to sort through the dreamers and the doers. If you found the right opportunity for you and your family, do you consider yourself a doer?

What would it be worth to you to double your income and triple your time off this year?

Then we should meet, shouldn't we?

What does your schedule look like? I'd like to schedule you for one of our local briefings.

This will give you more details so you can see if this is a good fit for you. Is daytime or evening better?

Great! We have a briefing this (Wed. at noon). Let me schedule you in.

Are you a committed person, _____? If you are serious about a real opportunity, then you will want to be there!

Do you have a pen and paper handy? Write down my name, and here's my number:_____. _____, If for any reason you can't make it, please call me so I don't hold up everyone saying, "_____ will be here soon."

See you on _____.

If they ask you:
CAN YOU JUST EMAIL ME SOME INFORMATION?

I can, but let me tell you—the reason we have so many successful individuals in our company is because of the one-on-one attention we give our students. Wouldn't it be wise to get all of the facts before making a decision?

Great! Let's get together on _____. Let me give you the address.

Trade Shows

Trade shows are also a great source of lead generation. Make sure you go with a reputable company, one that can show you their history and track record. Promises for the future won't pay the rent; the fees are going to be the same. You want to make sure that they have the walk-through capacity so you'll get the numbers they're promising. One way is to get referrals and develop contacts at convention centers.

Convention centers also have a published list of all upcoming expo and trade shows in the area, so you can pick and choose the best ones. You'll also want to affiliate yourself with the local chamber of commerce and other networking groups, as they are a great source of what trade shows are coming to town and which ones have been most successful. Pick the ones that attract likeminded clients and individuals to your type of business. If you're involved in real estate investing, you don't want to invest in attending a wedding expo.

Trade shows can be an expensive lead source generation, so you might want to organize a group to co-op the event with you. Typically, the higher the cost, the larger the trade show. After splitting the cost up front, put together a schedule and divide the booth into shifts that each person can sign up for. You can split the leads by either collecting them all and dividing them evenly at the end of the show, or allowing each person who works a shift to keep the leads they collect. Regardless of the way the leads are divided, just make the process clear before the event so that everyone knows what is required of them in order to get the leads. Come with a good attitude and it will be reflected accordingly.

NOTES

Notes

Contacting and Inviting

Mastering Your Dialogue

When you first get started in this industry, it can be scary getting on the phone. You're nervous about messing up. One of the best ways to get over this fear (or if you ever feel like you're running out of leads) is to pull out the yellow pages and start calling businesses. Try to make at least twenty calls a day, spending no more than five minutes on each phone call. If you do this five days a week, that's 100 calls. There is a 20 percent success rate in network marketing, so if you want to increase the number of people who look at your enterprise, then just increase those dials. You want to have a full calendar of people to call. When you sit down to make your calls, be prepared with all the contact information in front of you so when you're in your groove you won't be interrupted by having to locate a phone number.

Once you start generating leads, you'll contact and invite those individuals to meet with you at an event. The most important purpose of this event is to expose your best prospects in a nonthreatening way to your incredible opportunity. These people represent your Chicken List: friends, business associates, past and current prospects, etc. You can continue to generate local leads from any of your previous sources. Once you have prospects to call, you will begin to set up phone interviews with these individuals.

Contact them for live presentations, conference calls, and Webinars. Whatever the format, there is a lot of commonality and just a little bit of difference in how you commit them to your business exposure.

Keep in mind that one of the most important things you can do is to learn this information and then apply it to your personality. Dialogue is king—make it your own! When you make your calls, be enthusiastic over the phone. Smile! This will definitely be reflected over the phone. People can tell if you're being sincere or not. Don't go into an overload of information about your particular product. Keep it simple and short, and give them the key reasons for your product. This initial contact is to invite and make an appointment for them to attend a presentation or to meet with you one-on-one. No matter what though, you want to connect early on with your prospect, relaying to them over the phone why they want this product and how it is going to improve their current situation.

A person can become well-versed in the dialogue and language by doing it wrong enough for long enough. Practice, practice, practice! Role-play with someone else as if they're a real prospect. You can't stop in the middle of a presentation or conversation with an individual and say, "Wait, let me start over!" When I first started in this industry, my mentor would listen to me and tell me point blank how terrible I was. If you do it wrong long enough, you will finally get it right. Take the scripts that your company has and memorize them; learn them forwards and backwards. I've practiced in front of a mirror, my kids, and stuffed animals sitting on a chair. Rehearse it until it flows naturally, and then throw the script away.

It's so important to listen to your prospects and ask them qualifying questions to find out if this is even a person that you would want to work with, and if this is a person who is looking for your opportunity.

Getting the Commitment

When you've asked someone to be at a meeting, you want to make sure that they are committed to being there. Ask them if they are good at keeping their appointments. Will they be there? Are they committed to be there? If they don't show up, call them and ask them if they would like you to contact them again. Remember that less is more on the phone; you want to get to the point and get them committed. You don't want to be too vague or they won't show up, but at the same time, you don't want to give them too much information. Diarrhea of the mouth and constipation of the brain means that you will get them committed and then uncommitted in the same breath.

When speaking to your warm market, you can make the assumption that they will be there. Out of respect for your friendship, they will probably be willing to check out the opportunity you're offering to them.

You'll learn to become more adept at hearing what they mean rather than what they say. Your posture is created from the confidence you exude, how much you believe in what you're doing, and how convinced you are that your business will benefit them. It's all about finding out first and foremost if they have the time, asking them some questions about where they're at, and giving them some time to loosen up a little bit. After this, you can get right to the meat of it and tell them about what your company has to offer and share some success stories. Talk about what your mentors and other individuals have done and the success you've been witness to. This softens people's resistance and encourages curiosity.

Your goal is to get a solid 100 percent commitment, or else you have failed in the interview. Do not accept lame excuses. This means they will not show up. For you to get a solid commitment, you must ask solid questions. For example: "How good are you at keeping your appointments? Please be excellent at keeping this one!" Until you have that kind of forceful, solid "I will be there," you haven't set the appointment.

Out of those people who do commit, only about a third of them will actually show up. So, if you look at the glass as half empty instead of half full, you'll have a two-thirds no show ratio. It's a number game—don't fool yourself into thinking that because you've invited a certain number of people they'll all show up.

When I first started in my enterprise, I was invited thirteen times before I finally went to my first meeting. You must be compelling enough in your first invitation and bold enough to tell them to cancel whatever else it is that they have so that they can take a look at an opportunity that could change their life. You must have a high level of expectation. You're going to create a level of curiosity and have a level of confidence to push people to do something that they otherwise wouldn't do. If you're wishy-washy and weak in your approach, why should they keep the appointment?

They're going to blow you off. It's all the way you tell the story and get the commitment. They want to know there is something in it for them to come and meet with you.

It boils down to telling the story and controlling the conversation by asking the questions. The prospect controls the conversation by asking you questions and forcing you to do all the talking. You want to posture yourself according to the individual. If they're a cut-to-the-chase kind of individual, you'd better get to the point, and keep going back to the point and reiterating it. When someone asks me to cut to the chase and get to what this is all about, I let them know that this is an interview and they're not doing very well, and I ask them if they would like me to continue. This allows me to take control of the conversation again, and we'll either continue the conversation, or we'll end it and I'll move on to someone else.

The Importance of Posture, Urgency, and Curiosity

Your posture is extremely important. You must present yourself correctly, with the posture to be the leader that someone is going to want to collaborate with. You have to expect every person to take your opportunity seriously. Your posture depends on how seriously you take your own opportunity. There are three reasons why someone doesn't get involved in an opportunity: they don't believe in you; they don't believe in the opportunity; or they don't believe in themselves. Let's make sure that the only issue is *them*, because that we can assist them with.

Creating urgency is key. You never want to let someone know that you do a meeting at the same time every week. If you ever give them the perception that they could come any week, it will take them four months to get to a meeting. Create the urgency that this is a one shot deal and if they miss it, they will miss it forever. Anything you can do to create urgency increases the number of prospects that you'll have at an event.

Develop skill at hearing what people mean rather than what they say. If someone says they don't have the money, it isn't that they don't have the money. It really means that they don't find enough value in the product. If they say, "I'll try," it means "I'm not committed." These individuals are politely stepping out of the invitation. Don't chase people.

Learn to build curiosity. Less is more. Don't get into massive detail over the phone. Leave the door open for more information so your prospects will want to meet with you directly. Be very selective in the amount of information that you share with a person in your first interaction. Develop your skill at overcoming objections. Get good at one-liners. When someone tells me they just don't have business experience, I'll shoot right back at them, "Perfect, you're the exact person I'm looking for. Ignorance on fire is better than knowledge on ice. If you've got a work ethic and a desire to succeed, then I can assist you with the rest."

Continue to build curiosity, build urgency, and then secure a commitment. If your no show ratio is high, then you must figure out what you're saying on the phone and correct it, because in some way you're not creating curiosity, creating urgency, and getting your prospects to commit to an appointment.

Reconfirming the Appointment

Always reconfirm the appointment after someone has committed. Call them twenty-four hours before the appointment to make sure they are still planning to attend. One way I do this is to call them up to double-check the spelling their last name, or to make sure I gave them the address. You can also find someone you trust and have them call your prospects to confirm the appointment.

Let's review the steps to contact and invite someone to a meeting:

• Memorize your scripts so you know them forwards and backwards. Then throw them away and don't look at them again so you speak with confidence.
• Speak to your prospects as if they are friends; otherwise, it is a dead giveaway that you don't know them.
• Whatever you do, keep it conversational. You never want to sound like a telemarketer. * Qualify a prospect for your time. Get a prospect's permission to move forward.

• Ask good, probing questions. Write the answers down. I keep mine on a 3x5 card. Here I keep an overview, dates, and times so that I can access the information a moment's notice.

• When you're asked to share, be short and get to the point. Don't drag it out—remember that less is more. You can talk someone right in and right out of the business in the same conversation.

• Weave in your story and the stories of other people. Facts tell and stories sell.

• Speak with authority. This is called posture. You're not born with this; it is acquired over time. If you speak with authority and sell yourself first, this is what people will buy. If you want to make a little bit of money in your enterprise, then sell the product. If you want to make a little more money, than sell the product along with the opportunity. But if you want to be filthy, stinking rich, sell yourself. This is what your prospects are buying. They're asking themselves if you're the leader they're looking for.

• Remember to use different techniques to create urgency. Create the feeling of potential loss in your prospects.

• Before you get off the phone, get a solid, 110% commitment from your prospect, whether to review information, be at a meeting, meet you in person, or visit an online Webinar.

• Call and reconfirm the appointment.

Following Up after the Appointment

Try to follow up with a prospect within twenty-four hours after the scheduled appointment. Remember, the sooner the better. If possible, try to follow up with them the same day and then get them committed to attending the next event.

Here's an example of what I say to people when following up:

"Hi, _____, this is___. Have you got a minute? I'm just calling to get some feedback from last night. I'd like to ask you a few questions that will give me a feel for how we can improve our seminar. Is that okay?

"Did you feel that the information was presented in a credible fashion?

"After attending our seminar and learning about our marketing system, did you feel this opportunity would work for you? Why or why not?

"Is there anything we could have done last night that would have encouraged you to become a part of our team?

"What is your present interest in learning more about our opportunity?"

If the response is positive, then book an appointment to meet with them ASAP. If they are willing to meet with you, you have more than a 50 percent shot at bringing them on board.

Keep your approach simple and to the point. Be enthusiastic, and remember that ignorance on fire is a whole lot better than knowledge on ice. Rehearse these scripts until they flow easily. Get creative, and leave no stone unturned.

NOTES

The Details

Overcoming Adversity

It's worth it to work consistently in your new enterprise. It's important to develop momentum, because this is what will attract people into your enterprise. If you find yourself getting disheartened or slowing down after your first couple of months, then step up your game! Remind yourself that you are on the path to creating financial freedom for not only yourself, but everyone else that joins you along the way... that is, if they're willing to duplicate this same system and get into the game!!

Know beforehand that you will encounter negative people and scenarios; this is a part of the journey. Prepare yourself beforehand by telling yourself that you will not be offended or upset by negative responses. Persevere and know that you will be rewarded for hard and consistent work. All it takes is one key player to come into your enterprise for things to completely turn around. Part of being successful is being prepared to handle rejection along the way. If you know this is going to happen, you won't let it trip you up along the way. You'll find that as your experience increases so will your success ratios.

You first must learn what works and what doesn't; this is how you become more practiced and experienced. Remember, all you have to do is to "do it wrong enough long enough before you get it right."

If you feel that you aren't getting the appointments or responses that you had anticipated, then be strong enough to question your techniques and face into where you require improvement. Figure out how you can connect with people sincerely. You can't change other people, but you yourself can adapt and grow and progress. The most successful businesspeople I've had the opportunity to

collaborate with are constantly looking for areas to improve in, and then they put those plans into action!

You will get better the more you just do it! Practice doesn't always make perfect; however, perfect and objective practice does. You have to make the calls and get that appointment book filled. If you don't do it, NO ONE ELSE WILL! People are not going to call you up and ask you about your enterprise. You have to initiate sharing your opportunity with people.

Patience is such a vital aspect in the game of free enterprise and direct sales. It can sometimes take a year or more before you notice any real success. The reason most marketers fail is that they didn't have the patience and commitment to consistently promote their business for as long as it takes.

Tracking Your Progress

When results are measured, they will improve. It is critical for you to measure your own productivity. Become your own biggest competitor! If you create challenges and goals measured against your own productivity, your path to success will be greatly shortened. It is critical that you track and monitor your own productivity. This is the best way to remain consistent in your actions and to hold yourself accountable.

Often someone tells me that they're working their business to death but have nothing to show for it. I'll ask them to show me how they've tracked their production, and nine times out of ten they don't do that. That's when I ask them, "Are you wisely and consistently investing your time in money-producing activities for your business, or are you merely wasting time getting ready to get ready?" Don't worry about anything else, just focus on the activities that will bring you money. That's the bottom line! Tracking your progress will assist you in doing that.

Below is a low-tech, high-check way to create results—a printout you'll want to have for each day of your workweek. You can keep this on 3x5 cards, or put six on a page so you can keep them in a notebook. It's very simplistic—there is a blank copy for you to reprint and an example that shows lines each time you make a phone call or set an appointment or do a moneymaking activity.

You'll want to fill one of these out every day.

Daily

NAME: _____

Date: _____

Number Talked to: _____

Number Left Msg: _____

Appts. Set: _____

Number of Guests: _____

Events Attended: _____

Number of Follow-ups: _____

Lead Sources: _____

Daily - Example

NAME: _____ **Chad Wade** _____

Date: _____ **June 26** _____

Number Talked to: ~~IIII IIII IIII IIII IIII~~

Number Left Msg: ~~IIII IIII IIII IIII~~ II

Appts. Set: ~~IIII IIII IIII IIII~~ I

Number of Guests: ~~IIII IIII IIII~~ III

Events Attended: ~~IIII IIII IIII~~

Number of Follow-ups: II

Lead Sources: **12**

Below is an example of a report, so at the end of the week you can quickly see your results.

The top section is where you'll put your goals and the section right below it is your actual numbers. Keep track of the number of books/audios you listen to and read, the number of events you attend, and the number of lead sources you're utilizing.

The Lead Pool tracks how many good, solid leads you're working with each week.

The Meeting Pool tracks how many guests you intend to have at meetings that week.

Follow Up tracks how many people you plan to follow-up with each week and Sign Up tracks how many new people you'll sign up.

Certification shows how many people have signed up with you that you're now assisting in the certification process.

I can look at this Tracker and see where you're weak in about thirty seconds. If you have fifteen people booked for meetings and no one shows up, I know you require improved skills on the phone. If you've invited fifteen people and seven showed up, that is a normal ratio.

Of the seven that showed up, if there are no follow-ups being done, then I know that you're not booking them from one event to the next. They require that second exposure in order to get their questions answered, get third party credibility, and have you show them the power of your compensation plan again.... and then collect their decision to join you!

Always assume the sale. I expect that everyone who answers my ad, who shows up to a meeting, or who goes to a follow up will buy from me—and they do.

CRACKING the PRODUCERS CODE

Week _____   **Reporting** _____ / **200__**

Whatever the mind of man can conceive and believe, it can achieve! - Napoleon Hill

Goals

Book / Audio	Event #	Lead Sources #	Lead Pool #	Meeting Pool #	Follow Up #	Sign Up Pool #	Certification Pool #
Real Numbers	Real Numbers	Real Numbers	Real Numbers	Real Numbers	Real Numbers	Real Numbers	Real Numbers

When results are measured they WILL improve!

Refer to your goals above, and plan daily activities necessary to reach your goals.

1 to 10	Name	Phone Number	E-mail	Progression				
				1-1st contact	2-Conf call	3-Meeting	4-follow up	5-signed up
7	John Doe	801-555-5555	john@msn.com	6/10 1	6/14 2	6/16 3	6/19 4	6/19 5

It's important that you not only track your own success, but that you compare your success ratios to those who are pushing harder, creating more results, and making more money than you. Do you want to compare yourself to the best or to the worst?

When I was in high school, I ran on the track team. At practice, there was one kid in particular that was much faster than me in short-term sprints. By timing myself and comparing myself to his time and pushing harder to match his time, I went from being an average sprinter to one of the fastest on the team.

When I was on the wrestling team, during my first year I wrestled with kids who were two and three years older than me. They were bigger and stronger than me, and every day at practice I got my butt kicked. This made me try even harder and work harder, and when it came time for the big wrestling match, I took first place with ease.

When I look back at this, I succeeded because I compared myself to the best, the people around me were bigger and stronger, and I had to fight tooth and toenail to keep up with them. The next year, the same kids I had been hanging out with moved onto the next class, while I was forced to remain behind wrestling kids of my same weight. I was a little stronger than them, so I dominated at practice every day. But when it came time for that same competition, I got taken out on the first round, because I didn't measure my success, I didn't compare myself to the best, and in return, I didn't achieve the results of the past year.

FUN

You can have a blast creating team-building events. It is so important to create fun in order to develop unity and inspire people to take action. If it's not fun, it's work.

Leadership teaches you about people. If you turn around and no one is following you, then you're not a leader yet. I'm always looking for an excuse to get people together and to have fun.

Building an enterprise takes work, perseverance, and a lot of no's, but if you can have fun at the same time, you'll turn around and see people following you.

I get my team together often, whether it's for business or just to have some time to connect. I'll occasionally host a BBQ where my team can bring their family and friends. There's no presentation attached; it's just a great time for everyone involved. I always make it a point to invite all the significant others. These individuals are often your team members' backbones. It's very important to have their support, and a social event lets them know that you support them and appreciate them. It's a wonderful opportunity to promote unity.

Over the years I've developed my very best friends from my enterprise. A fun event is a way to get out and bond outside of the business arena. Every winter I get together with some of the other leaders on my team and we all go snowmobiling. It is a blast to get everyone together, bring their significant others, and just get out in the great outdoors and have a blast. Another example is introducing a little bit of healthy competition. I'll host contests with other members of my team to see who can drive the most business, whether it's passing out the most flyers, making the most phone calls, or getting the most guests to an event. We'll set it up so that the prize is something fun that everyone wants to receive. Oftentimes it will be an overnight stay at a local resort. A little bit of competition is a healthy way to motivate people and bring some fun into what we do!

NOTES

Taking Charge

Leadership Roles and Responsibility

You must be able to drive your personal income while developing and growing your team. You lead by example, so driving your income is critical to your success. For example, when you first get on a plane, the flight attendant says, "In the event of an emergency, put your oxygen mask on first, before you put it on a child or someone else." You've got to be able to take care of yourself first before you can take care of others.

A good leader sets the pace. Get to work and keep the pace going. I've made the money because I've put my nose to the grindstone. If you set the pace yourself, then you can require your team to put in a two-year commitment. Require them to roll up their sleeves and get to work.

Our emotions are often tied to our bank account, and if this is the case, it can really be discouraging and cause you to question your competency. So, focus on your sales first. Sales keep you motivated and in the mindset to lead others. Never put your income in the hands of other people's efforts. My income is a direct result of my desire to create my success and to assist other people to create their own success.

It all comes down to personal production. A broke person can't assist a broke person. You can't lead someone to higher ground if you're down on the ground yourself.

Don't start thinking that you only care about yourself. This is part of the sales cycle. You must create income for yourself; otherwise you'll never have credibility and be able to lead others. You have to set the pace. One of your primary functions is to assist the people you bring in to become independent as quickly as possible. This will free up more of your time for production as well.

There is one-on-one time, and there is group time that you can invest in with your team. I only invest the one-on-one time with people who deserve it. Not those who *need* it, those who *deserve* it. Group time is support that's available at presentations, trainings, and meetings.

Remember the gentleman that introduced me to my current marketplace? Guess what he did for me? NOTHING! That was the very best thing he could have done. When I called him to assist me with some calls, he told me that he didn't have time for me. This forced me to learn and do by myself. It put me in a leadership position, because I didn't have a crutch to lean on. It truly was the greatest gift he could have given me. Some of the biggest leaders in my enterprise have been trained by me, but it wasn't because they showed up empty-handed or expected me to train them. They got out there and did the legwork and training on their own. They brought people to the presentations, and then they came to me after they took action and asked me to assist them with closing and overcoming objections.

If you bring people to actual trainings and events, you'll get the best real-time training possible. I only give my one-on-one time to a select few. These are the people who are following through and taking action first. I make calls with those people. The most impressive thing is that they'll show up with a tape recorder and pad of paper and pen so that they can study and learn from this real-life training.

You absolutely must adopt as your personal motto, "If it is to be, it's up to me!" Realize the power you have in growing from student to teacher, from teacher to leader—all the while driving your personal business.

Creating a New Market

Many of you are going to be creating a new market for yourself. The geographic area that you're in may be small, and there might only be a couple of people in your organization. This means that you will be required to be the leader that gets the ball rolling.

A simple formula to follow is this: One-on-one presentations feed the home meetings, and home meetings feed people into regional and national conferences. If your numbers in attendance lack in any of these areas, look at the original source and go to work in that area. For instance, if your home meetings are poorly attended, it's because you have not enrolled enough committed associates to assist you with building for group presentations. You must start over with one-on-one presentations, and when your group is strong enough, you will then want to teach them how to build for group events. This formula can be applied wherever there is a weakness in your business.

When breaking ground in a new market, start with one-on-one presentations and build until you have enough associates to host a good home meeting. This can and should happen very quickly. Within the first week or two, you should start building towards this event. It is especially important at this time to keep your foot on the gas, as momentum will start to kick in and your efforts will be now compounded by the efforts of those on your team. As soon as you have about thirty-five to forty people attending your home or lunch meetings on a regular basis, it is time to secure a hotel meeting room on a weekly basis.

Be sure of your commitment before making this step. You will require the support of every committed associate to make this work, so establish a co-op first. The reasons are simple. It can become very expensive if the costs are not shared between a co-op of associates, and your meetings will become counterproductive if new guests are not in attendance each week. Every serious leader will have guests at these weekly events.

Assign one person the responsibility of coordinating with the hotel and signing any contracts. Shop around for a location that will provide easy access for all who attend, ideally one with freeway access. Look for a new, clean, and professional environment, but don't get carried away. Costs vary widely depending on the city and location. Smaller meeting rooms can range from $50 to $300 a week. When your guests reach over 100, the cost will go up as well, usually in the $150 to $300 per night range. When your numbers are over 250, your costs take another big leap. At this point, you are usually forced to meet at a larger hotel, and they can take you hostage if you're not careful.

Talk with the meeting and sales department manager. Let them know you will be meeting in their hotel weekly and you're not afraid to commit to a number of weeks in advance. Also let them know your budget; they will usually work with you on the price. Always start low and shop around. I have seen prices from $200 to $400 a night for the same hotel. Everything is negotiable.

Some of you may be feeling a bit overwhelmed. Don't worry, long before the time your numbers force you into bigger hotels, you will be having monthly trainings in your area. You can charge anywhere from $15 to $50 per person for each training, so your total collection from these monthly events will cover the cost of the weekly meetings. This means that you can still make the meeting free for all guests. Always remember, the bigger the group, the bigger the paycheck. Believe me, it's worth it.

When you have a willing team holding hotel meetings on a weekly basis, here are a few tips to make it run smoothly.

1. Get there early and set up the room.

A product table should be set up at the front right hand side of the room. Use an empty cardboard box about six inches tall and wide enough to support the company products when it is opened for display. The box should be placed on the table and then draped with a tablecloth. Place the product on top. This creates a multi-tiered effect that will lift the product and create a more attractive display. Make sure that you have the right music playing—something high energy but non-offensive. Music fills the air with energy and prepares the room for the presenter.

2. Put out about 20 percent fewer chairs than required.

Stack the rest of the chairs in the back of the room. Bring them out only if necessary. It sends a much more positive signal to bring out chairs as guests arrive rather than have a number of empty seats, or even worse, to be putting away chairs. You want people to believe that you have more people than expected, instead of fewer.

3. Set up a registration table outside of the door to the meeting room.

At least two associates should manage the table. Each person should sign in and be given a nametag. You can find these at office supply stores. Purchase them in two colors: one for guests and the other for associates. Nametags make it easier for associates and guests to find each other, the presenter will be able to interact with the audience by name, and guests can be introduced to more associates if nametags are in place. A sign-in sheet should also be present.

Make sure that it contains info like Name, Guest of, and Phone Number. It is always good to have the proper documentation if a guest of one associate gets recruited by another associate. It doesn't happen often, but when it does you can act quickly against those who may not be playing by the rules.

4. Greeters play a big role in the success of a meeting.

If at all possible, associates should accompany their guests to the meeting, but this is not always the case. When a guest shows up unattended, you want them to feel welcome and cared for. If a greeter can offer a handshake and a smile and guide them to their seat, it makes for a much more positive impression than if they show up to an indifferent or unfriendly crowd.

It can make the difference between a prospect getting excited about your opportunity or bolting for the door when the meeting is over. Strive to create an atmosphere of acceptance and belonging; it shows a spirit of unity and trust. It also sends the message that your team watches out for each other, even when there is no possibility of compensation. Assign two or three people as greeters each week. These should be some of your best, most enthusiastic, and trusted people.

5. Appoint a host or hostess to welcome everyone with enthusiasm, get them into their seats, and then edify the presenter in such a way that every guest will feel as though they are being instructed by the best of the best.

A possible introduction may sound like this: "Good evening everyone, may I have your attention, please. It wasn't long ago that I occupied a seat in an orientation just like this one. I too came to see what all the excitement was about, with hopes that this might be the opportunity I had been looking for. Fortunately, it was, and that's why we are here. We ask that you keep your minds open to possibilities. Please hold your questions until the end, turn off any cell phones, and remain seated for the entire presentation. This shows respect and courtesy for both our guests and our presenter. I encourage you to take notes and listen carefully. The information you will hear tonight can change your life for the better, and the person presenting is one of the best in the industry! With this in mind, let's get started. We are all extremely privileged to have with us one of our company's top leaders. He/She has become a mentor to many in this room and is truly making a difference in the lives of people all across this country. Let's give a huge welcome to_____! _

6. *"You will never have a second chance to make a first impression."*

This is why your best presenters must give the presentation. This is not a popularity contest. The presenter should be an established leader, not the newest, latest, or greatest. This is not a training ground for new talent. These individuals should be comfortable, confident, and prepared. They can use a white board or some other visual presentation materials. You may want to invest in an overhead projector as you gain a larger audience. This can be purchased for about $200— don't go for the big fancy ones. Next, obtain a PowerPoint presentation from your company, or create your own if your company doesn't have one. You can use your laptop to project the PowerPoint onto a large screen or even a large white wall. It's great to have these presentations already set up because they will keep your presenter on track and involve the audience more in the presentation. "Tell me, I will forget. Show me, I will remember. Involve me, I will understand." Experienced presenters understand this and make it a part of each meeting.

New associates will have plenty of opportunities to hone their skills at one-on-ones and home meetings. When they are polished, they will be given stage time. This must be the adopted policy in each area, and each associate should understand that it is for the betterment of all. In those areas just getting started, the rule still applies that the best presenter should be in front of the room, but the standards are more relaxed while the local leadership goes through the curve.

7. A word to the audience.

You will see the same presentation, given in the same way, by the same people, week after week. It will get old at times, but you must not let it show. For the presenter to reach your guest, he or she requires your cooperation. This is a team effort. Make sure that you laugh at all the jokes, even if you have heard them a hundred times before. Remain enthusiastic and excited about the presentation at all times. One fired up and excited person can infuse excitement into the rest of the room, even if that room is totally flat. Enthusiasm is contagious—catch it and then pass it on. It can be the difference between a big check and no check.

8. The meeting after the meeting is more important than the meeting itself.

When the presentation ends, stay seated. Do not stand up. If you remain seated, so will your guest. This is the time to answer questions and overcome objections if you want to close the sale. Do not be afraid to ask for the order. Use this as a possible closing question: "Are you ready to start making money now?" or "Do you see any reason why you wouldn't want to get started tonight?" If they require a push, then introduce them to one of the other leaders for added credibility. Find someone they can relate to that has a great income story. When introducing your guest to any leader, be sure to edify that person, because you will empower that leader to have added influence over your guest. It will bump up your success rate, and the introduced leader now has an opening to edify *you* in front of your guest.

9. Never bring negatives to a meeting.

They do not belong there. Take any negatives upline, and do it in private. Negatives go upline, and positives go to everyone else. Certainly at times you will deal with challenges, but a meeting is not the place to address them. In the event that an associate shows up with an attitude, take them to a private spot, and educate them. Encourage them to get in touch with their director.

10. Once the presentation has begun, do not leave your seat.

This is critical to everyone's success. Your guest does not know who the associates are and who is seeing this business for the first time. If you walk out for whatever reason, it will plant doubt in the mind of your guest, as well as distract the presenter.

11. Refrain from talking during the presentation.

Find a seat—do not stand around the back of the room while the presentation is being given. The only exception to this rule is when there is standing room only.

12. Every one is required to be in the room for the presentation.

Associates and directors should not be in the lobby conducting their own meetings. Your team will duplicate you, so show them that there is no better place to be than in the meeting.

13. Business dress is required.

This is a business meeting, and it should be treated like one. Your goal is to create an atmosphere of professionalism. Jeans, cut-offs, shorts, or immodest clothing do not have any place at a business meeting.

14. At the conclusion of the presentation, the host thanks the presenter.

They will ask for another round of applause to show appreciation. The host may say something like this: "I believe that we have unquestionably the most powerful opportunity in America today. I also believe that documentation beats conversation. At this time, I would like to introduce you to a few of our directors and let them share their own stories."

You should have *prearranged* testimonials from three to five individuals prior to the meeting. Call them up one at a time. Each testimonial should be one to two minutes long.

A sample testimonial may sound like this: "Hello, my name is Chad Wade. My background is in the dry cleaning business. I spent many years working in my family's dry cleaning business in Salt Lake City, Utah. The income was okay, but the more I made, the more time away from my family I endured. I was looking for a business that would that would allow me to buy back my time. Thank goodness for this company! Since joining, my whole life has changed for the better. Now I work from home, and I start my days saying, "I get to, I choose to, I want to." I no longer fight traffic, and my outlook on the future has never been more optimistic. It does not get any better than this!"

Keep the testimonials short and sweet. Don't forget to mention any company disclaimers regarding income examples or health testimonials. To wrap up the meeting, the host will use the three-step close.

15. The three-step close is a very inoffensive way to close out the meeting and determine the interest level of the prospect on the table.

It goes something like this: "I believe the information that you have received is sufficient for a person to now make an intelligent and informed decision about our opportunity. You should find yourself in one of three categories. A person in the third category has the opinion that our opportunity may look great but isn't for them. To those people we say, best of luck, thanks for coming. If you're a person in category number two, you're an individual that likes what you see, but you have a few questions to be answered before you get started. That's great! Get with us afterwards, and we will be happy to spend whatever time is required with you. If you are in the first group and you don't want to let any grass grow under your feet, welcome to our team! We will be here to assist you with ordering your product, signing up, and getting started today. Congratulations on your decision to get involved! All we ask is that you allow the person that invited you to ask you a simple question: 'Are you a one, a two, or a three?' That's it!"

It is the host's responsibility to close out the meeting, say goodnight, and get the music playing again.

#16. Even though the meeting is over, stay focused on its purpose.

The primary purpose of the meeting is for your guests first and then the associates. With this in mind, make sure you introduce your guests to the leaders in the room. This means the leaders must be free to speak with guests. They cannot be tied up in conversation with existing associates or directors, those already in the business. Speaking to each other has its place, but not while guests are still in the room. Too often, I see leaders surrounded with associates after the meeting, their time and conversations monopolized by associates when there is a long line of guests waiting for answers to their questions. Please be courteous to those you have invited to look into your opportunity. Save your questions until the guests have left the room. Then your leaders will be able to give you their full and undivided attention.

NOTES

NOTES

The Final Fifteen

This book contains a lot of information to get you on track with starting and becoming successful in network marketing and direct sales. Here are fifteen tips to keep you on the track to success. Print them out and hang them somewhere to assist you in remaining conscious of them, especially if you're new to the game!

1. **Be Enthusiastic; It's Contagious!** People will be drawn to your enthusiasm for your business. Get fired up and learn to stay that way. If you're talking to a prospect on the phone, stand up while you are talking, and project your excitement. If the meeting is in person, make sure your attitude is a positive one. I have always believed that for a business to be successful, you must be able to duplicate it, and it must be fueled by enthusiasm.

2. **The Three Cs of Recruiting: Compliment, Create Curiosity, and Get a Commitment.** It's been said that flattery will get you nowhere. I disagree. A sincere compliment can open a closed door almost every time. This is where you start when speaking to quality prospects. The next step is to create curiosity. You will only be effective at accomplishing this task if you remember to keep it simple and not give out too much information. Let the system do that. Curiosity is a powerful motivating force that, if used correctly, will drive your prospect from one event to the next and eventually into your business. One of my mentors said it best: "Say less to more people." Finally, you must get a commitment from your prospect, a commitment to read, listen, and investigate your business. Without a strong commitment from your prospect, you will only become frustrated because it will all be just lip service.

3. **Remember, You're Sorting, Not Selling!** Amateurs sell and professionals sort. "A man convinced against his will is of the same opinion still." I have experienced the frustration of recruiting people that I knew would be great in my business who didn't see it for themselves. Keep in mind that not every person you talk to will get involved on your timeline. Some will enroll today, others next week, next month, or next year—and some will never become involved. There are currently over 280 million people in the United States, so if the individual you are talking to doesn't express interest, say "Next," and move on to find someone that is ready today. If you find that you are contacting and re-contacting the same handful of people, your list of prospects is way too small. Make a bigger list and advertise more aggressively.

4. **Say No first!** With experience you will develop the ability to hear what people *mean* rather than what they *say*. Judge them by their actions as well as by the way in which they respond to your questions. Don't fall prey to those who give lip service but never take action. If you identify one of these people, say no first and move on.

5. **Facts Tell, but Stories Sell!** When asked what I do for a living, I have been known to respond, "I am the creator of success stories; are you next?" Rather than explain the features and benefits of my product, I know that that my message will be more readily accepted through a personal story, and it will also be remembered with greater accuracy. Words create pictures in the mind, and when they are put into story form, they enable your prospect to visualize more clearly. Sharing a personal experience creates credibility. That's why your own personal testimony of the product and the income opportunity are so important.

6. **Feel, Felt, Found.** These three words will enable you to overcome almost any objection. Here's how they work. Let's say you get hit with an objection: "I don't have any sales experience!" You respond, "Wow, I know just how you feel. I felt the same way, but let me tell you what I found out. I am not a salesman either, and I was terrified at the thought, but I learned that I would not have to be in the convincing business. I simply

share information and let my prospects decide. If they like what they hear through our conference calls or meetings, etc., then I direct them about how to get started. Does that sound like something you could do?"

You can apply the feel, felt, found method to almost any objection. If they say, "I don't have the time (the money, the education, or whatever), you respond with, "I know how you feel. I felt the same way, but let me tell you what I found out." It's that simple, and it allows you to convey your message through your own personal story. This will ease your prospect's fears and overcome their objection.

7. **Always Book a Meeting from a Meeting.** Never say to a prospect, "I'll get back to you." Make an appointment, and get a commit from them to keep it. When you ask them, "Are you good at keeping appointments?" they always say yes, and this gives you a chance to have them pull out their appointment book so that you can write it down together. Whatever the first meeting or phone call consisted of, always get an appointment for their next exposure. If you don't do this, you will end up chasing them about the next meeting—that kind of follow up turns into harassment and is usually followed up by a NO! There is a fine line between being persistent and being a pest. If you feel like you are chasing someone, stop. Move on to someone with a greater interest level.

8. **Follow Up within Twenty-Four to Forty-Eight Hours of Any Exposure.** Make your follow-up appointments within this time frame to continue an upward movement with your prospect's interest level. If you fail to make contact within this time frame, your guest will start to focus on all the reasons why they can't do this business instead of all the reasons why they should. The warm fuzzy feelings they felt with the conclusion of your previous discussions will go away, because life has a tendency to get in the way. Proper follow up is mandatory to building a healthy business.

9. **Use Third-Party Credibility Whenever Possible.** People like to do business with successful people. While you are building your own success story, lean on your successful leaders and their stories. After you have made a number of sales, you will have credibility to lend support to your associates, just as your leaders did for you. This cycle will perpetuate as your organization grows.

The other reasons for third-party support are these:
> * On-the-job training. You learn the details of your business from your upline as you participate with them on three-way calls, two-on-one meetings, etc.;
> * Your prospect gets a bigger picture of your opportunity when hearing about it from more individuals than just yourself;
> * Your prospect can get answers to any complicated questions;
> * I have observed that most people have to hear a second verification of the income opportunity from additional sources;
> * Your prospect will see that your upline assists you in becoming successful. They will be reassured that while they may be in business *for themselves,* they are not in *by themselves*;
> * Your leaders will be able to more objectively assess the interest of your guest;
> * Your leaders can get a commitment from your guest, assisting you to harvest the seeds you have planted.

10. **Put into the Three-Foot Rule into Daily Practice.** This business-building tip requires a little discipline. Whenever you are within three feet of someone, say hello and introduce yourself. Strike up a conversation and get a business card or phone number so you can introduce them to your incredible business. If you have planned ahead, you will have an audiocassette and a business card to exchange with them. It's that simple! So don't procrastinate. I am acquainted with many successful marketers that built empires by putting the three-foot rule into practice.

11. Avoid Four of These Five Stages of Business:

* Building mode: This is where you start, and this is where you should stay. This requires a commitment to lead by example. Commit yourself to personally enrolling new associates each month regardless of how large your organization gets. If you are not doing this, you will find that your business will come to a halt. Don't rely on qualifying sales to pay your bills. To be successful in your company, you must stay in the building mode.

* Management Mode: Unfortunately, many directors develop a false sense of security as soon as they have a few associates in their business. They movie into what we refer to as management mode. They believe that business will continue to boom as long as they simply provide support to those who are still working. If you catch yourself falling prey to this trap, look out! You will quickly find yourself without an organization or income.

* Defending Their Position Mode: This happens as a consequence of falling into Management Mode, or from trying to build a business against the proven plan of action. These are distributors who are attempting to justify their actions to their directors rather than conform to that which is proven. They try to reinvent the wheel.

* Blaming Mode: When a person starts to deal with the consequences of their own poor decision-making, they will often engage in blame transference. They blame everyone else for the lack of their success. It was their director's fault or the company's fault. They blame it on bad leads, inferior products, unprofessional conference calls, poor management, boring meetings, lack of training, the government, society, or alien beings from another world. Here is a word to the wise. Don't try to save these people. They have to figure it out on their own.

* Phase-Out Mode: By this time, a person has mentally checked out of the business. They have concluded that the opportunity does not work, or that it will not work for them. Because of their belief system, they just slip away into the shadows and you don't hear from them anymore.

The only way to avoid the chance of slipping into these different stages of failure is to STAY IN THE BULDING MODE.

12. **The Best Students Become the Best Teachers. Be the best!** Always be committed to learning and growing personally. Remain humble and teachable. This requires that you keep your ego in check and create in your mind the desire for increased knowledge and understanding.

13. **Remember, for Things to Change, You've Got to Change.** On the road to financial freedom, you must learn to conquer yourself. By our very nature, we as a race are resistant to change, but it is only through our willingness to submit to change that we will ever grow. Be flexible! Get out of your comfort zone! Learn to do more, be more, and dream more.

    We are all born equal, with the same opportunity to become unequal. Those who rise to great heights learn to embrace change, not fear it. Always be looking for a better way to approach your life and business. If a particular way doesn't work for you, find another, and another if necessary, but do not give up. Make a commitment to build this business *until*. Until what? Until you're done. Build it until.

14. **Time Management and the 80/20 Rule.** As you begin your business, your focus will be 100 percent directed towards personal recruiting. After becoming an associate, you will begin to develop your own marketing team. In the beginning this group will be small and manageable. Your time should be divided up: 20 percent towards assisting your new associates and 80 percent towards personal recruiting.

    This will gradually shift as your team becomes considerably larger. With a large and maturing organization, 80 percent of your time will be focused on training your team. They will learn best by the example you show them. Always dedicate 20 percent of your time towards personal enrolling efforts. This will ensure that you stay in the building mode. (My goal is to personally enroll at least six to eight new associates each month.)

I have learned though my own experience that 20 percent of your associates will account for 80 percent of your income, while 80 percent will account for 20 percent of your income. With this understanding, you can more easily identify you key leaders.

They are those individuals that possess the following attitudes:
* Burning desire to succeed
* Positive outlook
* Fun to be around
* Hard working
* Committed
* Teachable
* Confident
* Goal oriented

These individuals should be given 80 percent of the time you have set aside for your team. Give them one-on-one attention. On the other hand, the 80 percent crowd can be identified by many of these traits:
* Weak desire
* Negative attitude
* Complainers
* Lazy
* Not committed
* Not teachable
* Lacks confidence
* No goals

This group should only get 20 percent of your time, and even that should be spent in a group setting. Work with those that earn your time, not those that "need" it. Here is a clue: If you can't identify enough leaders in your group to spend 80 percent of your time with, then go build a new group!

15. **The Law of the Harvest.** Think of recruiting as a cooperative effort, much like farming. Before you can reap the rewards of the harvest, you must prepare the soil and plant the seeds. It is your responsibility to do the

weeding and planting; your upline's responsibility is to assist you with the harvest. The best time to involve your upline is after you've prequalified and exposed a prospect to your business, not before. It is not productive for you and your director to be making first contacts together (unless they are assisting you with your top twenty-five). That's your job. Follow the system, plant the seeds, plant more seeds, and then bring in your upline to harvest and close the sale. Because this is YOUR business, a proper attitude to adopt is, "If it is to be, it's up to me." Understanding each associate's role in the development of a healthy and growing business is a paramount to success.

NOTES

NOTES

15

Don't Let Anyone Take Your Bounce

Thank you for taking the time to read this book. I hope that it has given you insight and hope for the future of your business. You can do this—don't *ever* give up on your dreams! I want to share one last story with you before sending you out to take control of your business.

I was playing with my daughter on the trampoline one afternoon, when I got just a little too close to her. She quickly yelled out, "Dad, don't take my bounce!" Do you ever feel like people are taking your "bounce" by suggesting that what you are offering isn't really that great or telling you "that kind of money isn't possible"?

You've heard it before and I'll say it again, in this business we are underpaid until we are overpaid. **Networks take time to build.** Every successful distributor I have ever met understands that statement perfectly. They never let the word "no" bother them. They know that sticking with their business through the lean times is the only way to enjoy their business when things get better—and they *do* get better.

The problem is that we live our lives and run our businesses in a "demanding and instant society" that feeds on immediate gratification. Experts say modern Americans have a very short attention span. It's too easy to quit when our business temporarily slows down or a problem arises that seems too big to handle.

Thomas Edison is a great example of a man who could have very easily given up. He was a man with a very inventive and persistent mind; however, did you know that after failing many, many times, he concluded that it was impossible to put sound into movies? He gave up in 1915, and it only took a few more years before someone else figured out how to do it. Imagine how he felt! Even with that though, Thomas Edison gave us electric lights, and he invented the phonograph and movies. Over his lifetime, Thomas Edison had 1,039 patents!

When told he was a "genius," his response was, "Genius? Nothing! Sticking to it is genius! I've failed my way to success." Thomas Edison didn't give up, no matter what the situation or circumstance. He said, "I had to succeed because I finally ran out of things that wouldn't work." Ignorance on fire is better than knowledge on ice! If there is only one thing you learn from this book, it is that you take the information and keep applying the steps over and over until you finally reach a level of success.

I can attribute 100 percent of my success to copying other people's success one step at a time. If you eat a hamburger today, will it kill you? No! However, that same mistake repeated over time will be devastating to your arteries, and you could die of a massive heart attack. If you do not apply the information in this book today, will it kill you? No! But that same mistake repeated over time will be financially devastating to your direct sales and network marketing businesses.

When your mind begins to become clouded with doubt, it's important to remember what happens to those, even Thomas Edison, who gave up too soon! Another classic example is John Pemberton – a name you probably have never heard. He was a pharmacist out of Atlanta, and he had been successfully selling his headache remedy sweetened with French wine to people in town for quite awhile. Then in 1886, the city passed an alcohol prohibition ordinance that brought his sales to a screeching halt.

He made some changes to his formula, eliminated the wine, and came up with a syrup that could be sold as a fountain drink. Unfortunately, sales were not exactly earthshaking. By the end of the year Pemberton had earned just $50 in sales.

Pemberton found several investors and incorporated the company but soon gave up. He sold his shares in the new company and returned to making his patent medicine. He was so blinded by his current problem that he could not see the potential of this new formula he had created. Instead, he went back to what he already knew.

Asa Greggs Candler took over the struggling fountain drink business with a different vision: Why not sell the product in bottles? In less than ten years, Candler was successfully selling the popular drink in every state and parts of Canada. The original inventor, Pemberton, died in 1888 without knowing how wildly successful his formula for Coca-Cola would become worldwide.

Not all of us can be an Edison, but we can all avoid being a Pemberton. Don't give up! And don't let anyone take your bounce!

NOTES

Conclusion

You didn't really think it was over, did you?

Do you really want to guarantee your success? Do you want to name your next child after me? How bad do you really want it?

Then you'd better pay attention!

These are the rules of the game; you're either in or out. No benchwarmers allowed. It's your choice!

1.   Never miss a meeting, even if you have to crawl over broken glass in cutoffs to get there.

2.   Purchase your product or go home.

3.   Tell everyone about the "Greatest Opportunity in the World," even if you're alone.

4.   Practice your story until you can recite it backwards.

5.   Build up and edify everyone in your community. If no one edifies you, edify yourself!

6.   Support your team at all costs. If a team member calls you seven times a day, accept the call as if it were the first.

7.   Always respect the presenter. Laugh at all their jokes and stand up and cheer when they are finished with their presentation, even if the cheer is in gratitude for simply finishing.

8. Be able to present your company's compensation plan on a cocktail napkin at a bar. Warning: drinking during the presentation of the compensation plan can severely hamper your ability to sign anyone up.

9. Ask not what your mentor can do for you, but ask what you can do for your mentor.

10. Sign up eights, nines and tens with utmost effort—signing up multiples of threes, fours, and fives does not get the same results.

11. To stay in top physical condition, pick up the phone several times daily and make prospecting calls. Ten reps of ten phone calls is the recommended daily allowance.

12. If you aspire to be a leader in the community, be a follower first. Warning: once you are a leader, you must regularly turn around to see if anyone is following you. If you find no one is following you anymore, you must fall in line behind a leader, for you are now a follower again.

13. Never complain about anything your company is doing at any company event, in front of any prospect, ever! If you feel you must air dirty laundry after a meeting, you may feel free to do so in written format. Once the letter has been spell-checked and checked for grammatical errors, mail the letter to yourself, and immediately start working on a solution to the problem.

14. All prayers before meals and before bed must start with thanking God for your company and its owners... and my book.

15. If you're not waking up in the middle of the night saying, "Insert your company name here" in a cold sweat, you don't get it.

16. All newborns of marketers must be named Chad. If you don't plan on having any more children, nickname your current children Chad (parents of female children may use Chadette, Chadee, Chadina, or Chadry).

17. The three-foot rule is for rookies. The players use the ten-foot rule and regularly carry a soapbox and megaphone to deliver "The Story."

18. You must have fun in everything you do. The definition of fun for a marketer is selling your top package.

19. Average marketers walk with the walkers and think they run with the runners. Winners run with the runners and run over the walkers. To avoid being run over, RUN!

20. There are no free lunches for players. The responsibility of the "event" is for all that choose to market. No pay, no play. Continental breakfast not included.

21. Your system is the only system, and it is bigger than all of us. If anyone ever feels that the system is flawed, they need only to reflect on the system that brought them to the system and look at their own reflection to see the flaw.

22. Assisting others is why we are here. At first, you are introduced to the system by someone that wanted to assist you, but as soon as you make the conscious decision to join your enterprise, you are immediately converted from the helped to the helper!

23. Get used to giving people a slap and following it with a kiss. If you are ever confused about whether you should be slapping or kissing—slap twice to clear and then kiss.

24. Be sure to recognize your team for their results and commend them for their efforts. Warning: results and effort are required for this to work.

25. You should always be prospecting. If you spend any time wondering whether or not you are prospecting enough, you are obviously not prospecting enough.

26. There are amateurs, professionals, and players. Players make things happen, professionals watch things happen, and amateurs wonder what the heck happened! If you wonder a lot or watch a lot, you are not a player. Be a player!

27. To have, you must do. To do, you must be. Be-Do-Have, *NOT* Have-Do-Be.

28. Make mistakes as many times as you like, because mistakes have to happen before any success is achieved. Warning: A mistake done on purpose is vandalism – don't vandalize your success.

29. If you want to make money, sell your products. If you want to make a lot of money, sell the system. If you want to be wealthy, sell yourself (you might need to update yourself with the useful features first!).

30. You are paid in exact proportion to the value you bring to society. If you are not making anything, you should have a pretty good idea of your value.

31. The amount of money you make is exactly proportionate to the problems you can solve. To learn how to solve problems, you must practice solving your own problems first—personal development is essential to accomplish this.

WARNING: if you read this and are offended at any moment in time, you are not an eight, nine, or ten and MUST seek immediate help by hanging around more eights, nines, and tens!

All *complaints* may be sent to: <u>www. thisOPPORTUNITYisNOTright4U.com</u>

NOTES

NOTES

NOTES

Notes

NOTES

NOTES

NOTES

NOTES

_____

_____

_____

_____

_____

_____

_____

_____

_____

_____

_____

_____

_____

_____

_____

_____

_____

NOTES

_____

_____

_____

_____

_____

_____

_____

_____

_____

_____

_____

_____

_____

_____

_____

_____

_____

NOTES